THE
FAR·EAST
COOKBOOK

THE
FAR·EAST
COOKBOOK

More than 175 tantalizing recipes from the Far East

a Salamander book

Published by Salamander Books Limited
LONDON

a Salamander book

Published by Salamander Books Limited
129-137 York Way
London N7 9LG
United Kingdom

1 3 5 7 9 8 6 4 2

© Salamander Books Ltd. 1995

ISBN 0 86101 800 1

All correspondence concerning the content of this volume
should be addressed to Salamander Books Ltd.

Printed in Italy

CONTENTS

INTRODUCTION

The area loosely termed as the Far East, covers a vast expanse of the world. It is a fascinating area comprised of richly varied countries. There is, however, a core of similarities running through the cuisines of all the countries. They are all exciting, enticing and, to Westerners, have an exotic mystique.

They have broadly similar indigenous fruits and vegetables, rice is ubiquitous and spices are used extensively and cleverly to add zest to dishes and transform the same food so it tastes different from day to day. Spices and seasonings also have clearly defined attributes that are supposed to help the body in specific functions – ginger, for example, is considered a digestive. Throughout the region certain spices crop up time and time again, namely garlic, ginger, spring onions (scallions), soy products, and chillies.

Dips, chutneys, condiments, relishes and pickles have an important role on nearly every meal table. Dairy products are not used, meat is a luxury and desserts are rarely served (meals end with fresh fruit). Emphasis is placed on balancing spicy, hot flavours with cool ones; salty or sour tastes with sweetness.

In the Far East, diners sit at round tables, and most meals (banquets are the major exception) do not follow the Western structure of separate courses. Instead, dishes tend to be served simultaneously, or simply in the order in which they are cooked. One of the most exciting aspects of Far Eastern eating is that at every meal you get what amounts to a multi-choice meal because diners dip into dishes as they choose, taking a small portion to their plates or bowls to put on a bed of rice.

Together, the cuisines of the Far East compose a beguiling collection of many of the world's most appetising dishes, evolved over centuries. There is no need to eat only the dishes of just one country at a time. Have fun and feel free to prepare meals from whatever you fancy, juxtaposing a Japanese recipe with a Thai recipe, a Malay dish with a Chinese one, for example. However, it is best to precede a highly spiced dish with a more subtle one, not vice versa.

COOKING IN THE FAR EAST

Although there is a backbone of similarities between all the countries of the Far East, the diverse cuisines all have their own essential and unique characters.

CHINA

China is the largest of the Asian countries and it has the most varied landscape, climate and cultures. Inevitably, this has resulted in a number of different culinary styles. For example, in the north, where it is colder, wheat, not rice, is the staple and is used to make noodles, pancakes and dumplings. Dishes are more robust, and beef is more commonly eaten than elsewhere. In contrast, in the east around Shanghai, where the climate is milder, the land fertile and the seas and rivers provide fish and seafood, dishes are delicate and often slightly sweet; rice is used generously. The food of Sichuan, in the west, shows yet another contrast – the cooking is spiked with chillies and sweet-sour and salty combinations. Cantonese cooking, from the south, is linked with stir-frying, which grew out of a shortage of fuel (brief, hot cooking used less wood or coal). To be successful, stir-frying must be teamed with time-consuming chopping, slicing and dicing of the vegetables, poultry, meat or fish used in a dish.

JAPAN

Historically, Japan has remained isolated from its neighbours, so its cuisine has greater individuality. Flavours are more subtle than those of other Far Eastern countries, being typically clear, light and delicate; Japanese cooks believe that separate flavours should be shown in relief, rather than blended to a mellow whole. Harmony and balance are all-important.

Japanese dishes are characterized by elegant simplicity. Great attention is paid to the artistic, neat appearance of dishes, but not at the expense of the freshness or quality of the ingredients or the flavour of the food.

Until fairly recently, the Japanese diet was mainly a vegetarian one relieved by fish, which is still enjoyed raw as well as cooked.

KOREA

Koreans favour more pungent flavours, although their spice repertoire is fairly restricted. Garlic, chillies, ginger and spring onions (scallions) are used generously. Soy sauce, sesame oil and seeds, often toasted and crushed with salt, also make frequent appearances.

SOUTH-EAST ASIA

The countries of South-East Asia – Thailand, Malaysia, the Philippines, and Indonesia – share common flavourings beyond the Far Eastern ones – lemon grass, garlic, chillies, fermented seafood pastes and sauces. Richness in sauces comes not from dairy products but coconut milk and cream, while nuts are ground to a paste to thicken and enrich. Satays and curries are common throughout the region. Although ingredients are the same throughout South-East Asia, each country has its own way of preparing and serving them.

THAILAND
Thai dishes are made fragrant and flavourful by a glorious array of aromatics – bright galangal, tangy citrusy limes and the more subtle lemon fragrance of lemon grass, heady basil, fiery chillies, and garlic. Savoury dishes are characterized by a subtle sweetness, resulting from the addition of palm sugar. The appearance of dishes matters more to Thais than to other South-East Asians but Thai cuisine has the least European influence. Instead, Chinese and Indian influences are noticeable both in the cooking methods and the ingredients. But in Thai hands they have a new, sophisticated profile. Stir-fries are not thickened with cornflour as they are in China, so are lighter and fresher tasting. Unlike Indian curries, Thai curries are cooked quickly and lack the rich heaviness that results from long slow simmering.

INDONESIA
The use of spices is a particularly notable characteristic of the Indonesian cuisine, for the famed 'Spice Islands' produce a treasure trove of exotic aromatics. Curries are important, but often the rich colour and flavour of soy sauce produce a curry with a very different and distinctive taste. Sauces are also important. They may be thin and fiery, thick and nutty, oily and spicy-sweet, or any combination of the above.

Dishes may be served hot, warm or at room temperature, but usually the latter. Condiments are a must, with soy sauce, chilli, shallot and seafood pastes the main ingredients of compound sauces, plus a rainbow of raw and pickled fruits and vegetables.

PHILIPPINES
The colourful cooking of the Philippine Islands is an exciting amalgam of many influences, principally Chinese, Indonesian, Malaysian and, unusually for South-East Asia, Spanish. The unique Felippino custom of 'merienda' has its roots in Spanish 'tapas', although it begins about 4 o'clock in the afternoon and combines a selection of small cakes and sweet dishes with savoury snacks, often served buffet-style, as is much of the food on the islands.

There is a sharpness and tartness running through much Felippino cooking which comes from the use of a citrus fruit, the kalamansi, that is halfway between a lime and a lemon, and palm vinegar.

INGREDIENTS

Bamboo shoots: Young tender shoots from the base of the bamboo shoots, these are crunchy but bland, absorbing stronger flavours. Sold canned.

Banana leaves: Used to make containers for steamed foods, to which they impart a delicate taste.

Bean curd: Known as tofu in Japanese, this is a nutritious low-calorie food made from soy beans. Bland, with a soft-cheese texture, it absorbs other flavours. Stir-fry with care as it can disintegrate. 'Silken tofu' has a much softer texture and is mostly used in soups and sauces.

Bean sprouts: These small, young tender shoots are usually mung beans that have germinated, although other beans can also be allowed to sprout. Bean sprouts are nutritious, containing generous amounts of vitamins and minerals, and add a delicious crunch to stir-fry dishes.

Black beans: These small, fermented soy beans are very salty. Black bean sauce, in cans or bottles, is a quick, handy substitute.

Bok choy: Also known as Chinese cabbage, this resembles Swiss chard.

Celery cabbage (wong ah bok): A delicate pale green vegetable with a sweet taste that makes it ideal for use in salads. Its delicate flavour blends superbly with other foods.

Chillies: Add flavour as well as 'hotness'. Thais favour small and very fiery 'bird's eye' chillies but elsewhere these are only available in specialist shops. Chillies are rarely labelled with the variety or an indication of 'hotness'; as a rule of thumb, smaller varieties are hotter than large ones. Dried chillies have a more earthy, fruity flavour. The seeds and white veins inside a chilli are not only hotter than the flesh, but have less flavour, and are generally removed before using. Chillies contain an oil that can make the eyes and even the skin sting, so wash your hands after preparing them and avoid touching the eyes or mouth.

Chinese beans: The tender pods of these green beans can be eaten whole.

1 galangal; 2 ginger root; 3 coriander; 4 Chinese black mushrooms; 5 chillies; 6 Thai sweet basil; 7 Thai holy basil.

Snap beans or French beans can be substituted.

Chinese black mushrooms: These dried mushrooms have quite a pronounced flavour amd must be soaked for 20-30 minutes before use. The stalks tend to be tough so are usually discarded. Available in Oriental food stores.

Chinese black vinegar: Black vinegars are made from grains other than rice, and aged to impart complex, smoky flavours with a light, pleasant bitterness. Substitute sherry, balsamic vinegar or a good red wine vinegar.

Choy sum (Chinese flowering cabbage): Very similar to 'bok choy', though slightly smaller, with narrower stalks and slightly paler green leaves; the distinctive feature is the yellow flowers. These are cooked with the rest of the vegetables.

Coconut cream: The layer that forms on the top of coconut milk.

Coconut milk: Not the liquid from inside a coconut, but extracted from shredded coconut flesh that has been soaked in water. Soak the shredded flesh of 1 medium coconut in 315 ml (10 fl oz/1¼ cups) boiling water for 30 minutes. Tip into a sieve lined with muslin or fine cotton and squeeze the cloth hard to extract as much liquid as possible. Coconut milk can also be made from unsweetened desiccated

coconut soaked in boiling water, or milk, which will be richer. Allow 315 ml (10 fl oz/1¼ cups) liquid to 225 g (8 oz/2⅔ cups) desiccated coconut. Put into a blender and mix for 1 minute. Refrigerate coconut milk.

Coriander leaves: Best bought in large bunches rather than small packets. Stand whole bunches in cold water in a cool place.

Coriander roots: Roots have a more muted taste than the leaves. Large coriander bunches sold in Middle Eastern stores often include the roots. Fresh roots will last for several days if kept wrapped in a cool place, or can be frozen. If unavailable, use coriander stalks.

Daikon: A long, white, bland root vegetable with a crunchy texture, also called mooli or Japanese white radish.

Fish sauce: Also called nuoc nam and nam pla, this is made from salted, fermented anchovies and used in sauces, stir-fries and as a condiment. It is rich in protein and B vitamins and is salty, but the flavour is mild. The lighter Vietnamese and Thai sauces are best. A little goes a long way.

Five-spice powder: A blend of cinnamon, cloves, star anise, fennel and Szechuan pepper, used in Chinese marinades and sauces. Sold in supermarkets and Asian markets.

Galangal: Also known as Thai ginger, laos and lengk haus. There are two varieties, lesser and greater; the latter is preferred and more likely to be found in the West. It looks similar to root ginger but the skin is thinner, paler, more translucent and tinged with pink. Its flavour is also similar to ginger but less hot and with definite seductive citrus, pine notes. To use, peel and thinly slice or chop. The whole root will keep for up to 2 weeks if wrapped in paper and kept in the cool drawer of the refrigerator, or it can be frozen. Allow to thaw just sufficiently to enable the amount required to be sliced off, then return the root to the freezer. Galangal is also sold dried as a powder or in slices, the latter giving the better flavour. Substitute 1 dried slice or 1 teaspoon powder to each 1 cm (½ in) used in a recipe; in recipes where fresh galangal is pounded with other spices, mix the dried form in after the pounding; elsewhere, use as normal.

Ginger root: This knobby root's sweet spicy flavour is used in oriental soups, stir-fries and in fish dishes. Choose firm, heavy pieces that have a slight sheen. Store in a dark place, but do not refrigerate, for up to a week.

Gingko nuts: These have a hard shell, which must be removed before cooking, and a creamy coloured flesh. Shelled gingko nuts are also available in cans. If unavailable, substitute almonds.

Hoisin sauce: A reddish brown sauce based on soy beans and flavoured with garlic, chillies and a combination of spices. Flavours vary between brands, but it is nearly always quite sweet and it can range from the thickness of a soft jam to a runny sauce. It is used in Chinese marinades, barbecue sauces and stir-fries.

Kaffir lime leaves: The smooth, dark green leaves give an aromatic, clean citrus-pine flavour and smell. They keep well in a cool place and can be frozen. Use ordinary lime peel if kaffir lime leaves are unavailable, substituting 1½ teaspoons finely grated peel for 1 kaffir lime leaf.

Lemon grass: A long, slim bulb with a lemon-citrus flavour. To use, bruise the stems, then cut off the root tip, peel off the tough outer layers and cut away the top part of stalk. The stalks will keep for several days in a cool place, or they can be chopped and frozen. If unavailable, use the grated rind of ½ lemon or a lime in place of 1 stalk.

Long beans: Although these can grow to over 1 metre (3 feet) it is best to use younger ones. Green beans or French beans can replace them.

Lychees: Canned lychees are easy to find in supermarkets, but fresh ones are now becoming far more readily available. They need no more preparation than using the fingers to easily crack the knobbly, brittle coating.

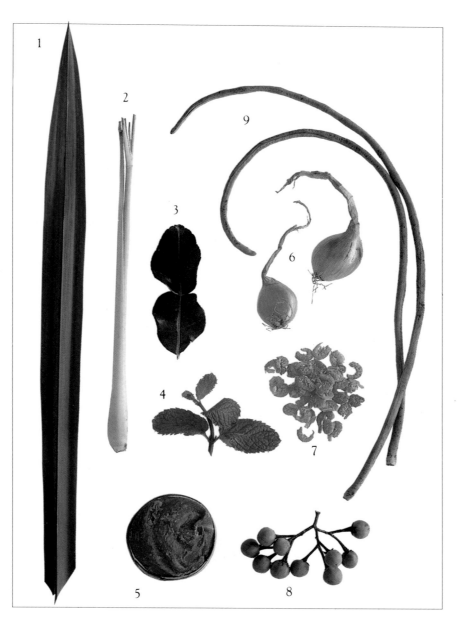

1 pandanus leaf; 2 lemon grass; 3 kaffir lime leaves; 4 Thai mint; 5 palm sugar; 6 shallots; 7 dried shrimp; 8 pea aubergines; 9 long beans.

Beneath it, delicious white flesh surrounds a smooth central stone.

Mango: There are many different types of mango, each one varying in size, shape and colour. Select fruit that feels heavy for its size and is free of bruises or damage. A ripe mango yields to gentle pressure and should have an enticing, scented aroma. The flesh inside should have a wonderful, luxurious and slightly exotic texture and flavour but poor quality fruit can be disappointing; the key is the fragrance. If a mango is a little firm when bought, leave it in a warm sunny place to finish ripening.

Mushrooms: Chinese cooks seldom buy fresh mushrooms, preferring to use dried ones. These must be soaked before cooking. Put the mushrooms into a bowl, cover with boiling water, cover the bowl, leave for about 20-30 minutes until swollen and pliable, then drain well. If the stems are tough, discard them.

Cloud ear: Also known as 'wood ear', these are added for their texture rather than flavour, as they have little.

Straw: These thin, tall, leaf-like mushrooms are also known as 'paddy straw' or 'grass' mushrooms. They are sold canned as well as dried.

Winter black mushrooms: With a fairly intense, fragrant flavour, these are the most widely used.

Noodles: Most types are interchangeable, but two, rice stick noodles and bean thread noodles, can be crisp-fried. Dried noodles are usually soaked in cold water for 10-20 minutes until softened, before cooking; in general, the weight will have doubled after soaking. After draining, the cooking will usually be brief.

Bean thread: Also called cellophane, mung bean, glass or shining noodles, these transparent noodles are made from ground mung beans. Stir into soups or stir-fry with vegetables. Soak in warm water for 5 minutes for general use, but use unsoaked in deep-frying.

Dried Chinese spaghetti: This thin firm noodle cooks quickly. Any thin spaghetti-type noodle can be substituted. Chinese egg noodles are also sold fresh in supermarkets and Asian markets.

Fresh rice noodles: Packaged cooked and wet in wide, pliable 'hanks'. To use, without unwinding, cut into ribbons and stir into a dish just to warm through.

Rice sticks: Long, thin dried noodles made from rice flour, rice sticks (also known as rice vermicelli) can be fried directly in hot oils and increase many times in volume. A good base for any Chinese-style dish.

Soba: This spaghetti-size noodle, made from buckwheat flour, is often used in Japanese soups. Ideal for cold noodle salads and very quick cooking.

Oriental aubergine: These long, thin aubergines are tastier than the large ones, do not need peeling and do not absorb much oil. Sold in supermarkets and Asian markets.

Oyster sauce: A thick, brown, bottled sauce with a rich, subtle flavour, made from concentrated oysters and soy sauce. Often used in beef and vegetable stir-fry dishes.

Palm sugar: Brown sugar with a slight caramelized flavour, sold in cakes. If unavailable, use granulated sugar and demerera sugar in equal proportions.

Pandanus (screwpine): Both the leaves and the distilled essence of the flowers, called kewra water or essence, are used to give an exotic, musky, grassy flavour to Thai sweet dishes.

Pea aubergine: Very small aubergines about the size of a pea, and usually the same colour, although they can be white, purple or yellow. The fresh, slightly bitter taste is used raw in hot sauces and cooked in curries.

Pickled and preserved vegetables: Various types of vegetables, preserved, or pickled, in salt, are availabe in cans and plastic pouches, but if a label simply specifies 'Preserved Vegetable', it will invariably mean mustard greens. 'Turnip' is not the Western variety, but a type of radish.

Plum sauce: A thick, sweet Cantonese condiment made from plums, apricots, garlic, chillies, sugar, vinegar and flavourings. Use as a dip or a base for barbecue sauces.

Rice: Thais mainly use a good quality variety of long-grain white rice called 'fragrant' rice. Ordinary long-grain white rice can be substituted. To cook, rinse the rice several times in cold running water. Put the rice into a heavy saucepan with 315 ml (10 fl oz/1¼ cups) water, cover and bring quicky to the boil. Uncover and stir vigorously until the water has evaporated. Reduce the heat to very low, cover the pan tightly with foil, then place on the lid. Steam for 20 minutes until the rice is tender, light, fluffy and every grain is separate.

'Sticky or 'glutinous' rice: An aptly named short, round grain variety. It can be formed into balls and eaten with fingers, or used for desserts.

Ground browned rice: Sometimes added to dishes to give extra texture. For this, dry-fry raw long-grain white rice until well-browned, then grind finely.

Rice vinegar: The mildest of all vinegars, with a sweet, delicate flavour and available in several varieties. If possible, use a pale rice vinegar for light-coloured sweet-and-

Above: *Chicken and Mushroom Rice (page 77).*

sour dishes, and try a dark variety for dipping sauces. If neither is available, use cider vinegar. Use Japanese rice vinegar for salad dressings, sauces, and pickling; Chinese vinegar is not strong enough.

Rice wine: Made from fermented rice and yeast, this mellow wine is widely used for stir-fry cooking. Similar to sherry in colour, bouquet and alcohol content (18%), but with its own distinctive flavour. If unavailable, substitute a good dry sherry.

Rose wine: Imparts an exotic quality to foods. Use sweet sherry as a substitute.

Sesame oil: Made from toasted sesame seeds, this has a rich, golden brown colour and a nutty flavour and aroma. Has a low smoking point and can burn easily. As a seasoning, a teaspoon added to a stir-fry dish just before serving adds a delicious flavour.

Sesame seeds: Widely available, these add texture and flavour to stir-fry dishes. Dry-fry in the wok first to bring out flavour, then stir-fry and use as a garnish. Black sesame seeds can be interchanged with white ones – dry-fry them in the same way.

Shallots: Thai red shallots are smaller than Western ones. They have quite

a pronounced flavour that is almost fruity rather than pungent. Ordinary shallots can be substituted.

Shrimps, dried: Whole dried shrimps are used to add texture and flavour.

Shrimp paste: A pungent, salty paste that is packed in jars, cans and plastic packets. Keep in a cool place.

Soy sauces: This essential Chinese condiment, flavouring and dipping sauce is made from a fermented mixture of soy beans, flour and water. The more delicate light soy sauce is most common. It is salty, but can be diluted with water. Dark soy sauce is thicker and sweeter, containing molasses or caramel. Japanese soy sauce, shoyu, is always naturally fermented.

Spring roll skins: These paper-thin, flour-dough skins are sold as Shanghai wrappers or lumpia skins. They are thinner and fry more crisply than thicker Cantonese egg roll skins. They can be refrozen.

Star anise: This eight-pointed star-shaped pod has a mild liquorice flavour and is used in marinades.

Star fruit: Star fruit, also known as carambola, are long, almost translucent yellow, ridged fruit. The whole

fruit is edible, and when cut across the width, the slices resemble five-pointed stars. Raw star fruit have a pleasant, citrus-like, juicy sharpness, but when poached the flavour is more distinctive.

Szechuan peppercorns: These aromatic, reddish brown dried berries have a mildly spicy flavour. Toast in a dry wok or frying pan before grinding to a powder.

Tamarind: Sold in sticky brown-black blocks, tamarind provides a sharp, slightly fruity taste. To make tamarind water, break off a 25 g (1 oz) piece, pour over 315 ml (10 fl oz/1¼ cups) boiling water. Break up the lump with a spoon, then leave for about 30 minutes, stirring occasionally. Strain off the tamarind water, pressing on the pulp. Discard the remaining debris and keep the water in a jar in the refrigerator. Ready-to-use tamarind syrup can sometimes be bought; it is usually more concentrated, so less is required.

Thai basil: Also called 'holy basil', Thai basil leaves are darker and their flavour slightly deeper, less 'fresh', than ordinary sweet basil. Bundles of leaves can be frozen whole in a polythene bag for up to about 2 weeks; remove leaves as required and add straight to dishes. Substitute Thai sweet basil or ordinary sweet basil, if necessary.

Thai mint: This has a sweet flavour. If unavailable, Western spearmint or garden mint are the best substitutes.

Water chestnuts: A starchy, bland, crunchy tuber. Use raw in salads, or add to soups and stir-fries. Widely sold in cans; rinse in cold water, or drop briefly into boiling water then rinse, to remove any metallic taste.

Wonton skins: These smooth, wheat-flour dough wrappers about 7.5 cm (3 in) square are sold fresh and frozen in supermarkets and Asian markets.

Yellow bean paste/sauce: This thick, aromatic, spicy sauce is made from fermented yellow beans, flour and salt. It is used to flavour fish, poultry and vegetables.

EQUIPMENT

Cooks in the Far East often spend more time in the kitchen preparing the ingredients than cooking them. Cooking utensils are few, practical and versatile, and are designed to make the most efficient and economical use of heat.

Cleaver: Cooks in the Far East use a cleaver for all tasks that require a knife, from carving delicate flower shapes from vegetables to chopping bones. A chef will select the cleaver that has the right size and weight for his or her physique. Frequent honing on a stone ensures that it is always razor-sharp.

Chopsticks: Special long chopsticks are used for cooking, particularly stir-frying. For eating, pick up a chopstick as you would a pen or pencil, square ends pointing upwards and rounded or tapered ends downwards, and let an equal amount of the chopstick protrude on each side of the hand. Now, instead of holding the chopstick with your thumb and index finger, as you would hold a pencil, hold it with the tips of the fourth and the little finger and let the upper part of the chopstick rest comfortably in the base of the thumb and the index finger. This is the stationary chopstick. With your other hand, pick up the second chopstick and place it directly above the first, and parallel to it. Hold the upper stick firmly with the thumb, index and middle fingers as you would a pencil. Use the thumb to brace the stationary chopstick securely against the tip of the fourth finger. There should be about 2.5 cm (1 in) of space between the sticks. Press the upper chopstick down with the index and third finger so that it meets the stationary chopstick to pick up the food. Tap the ends of the chopsticks gently on the table to make sure they are even as they will not work efficiently unless aligned.

Pestle and mortar: Used during the preparation of the majority of savoury dishes. A small blender or coffee grinder kept specifically for the purpose will take away the effort but will not produce quite the same results. When used for fibrous ingredients such as galangal and lemon grass, the pestle and mortar crushes the fibres rather than cutting them and so

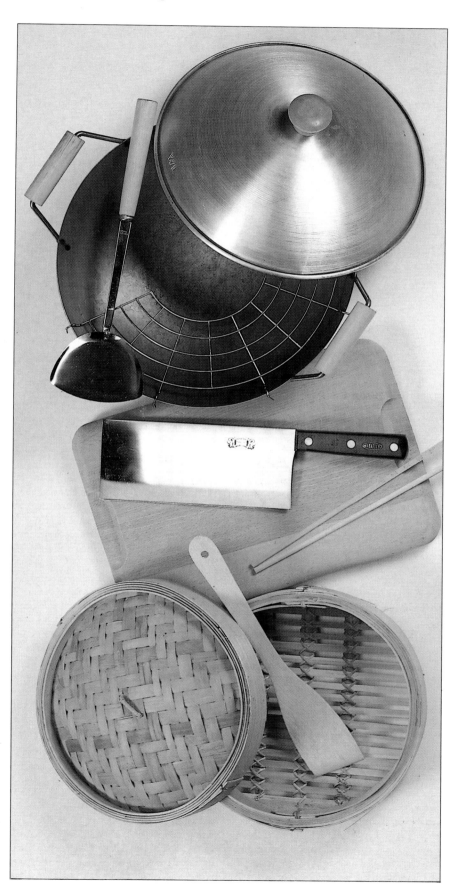

releases the flavour in juices and oils more successfully.

Rack: For using in a wok to support the steaming basket or container of food above the level of the water.

Skimmer: Shallow, wide, metal mesh skimmers are used for lifting deep-fried food from the oil, and for serving pieces of food from 'pot-style' meals.

Spatula: For efficiency, safety and comfort when stir-frying, a spatula with a curved blade that follows the contours of the wok, and a long handle that allows the hand to be kept away from the heat, is used.

Steamers: Bamboo steamers, designed to sit over a wok, are often stacked two or more high so that a number of dishes can be cooked at the same time. The steam is absorbed by the bamboo lid preventing water dripping on to the food. So that all the nourishing juices and flavour are retained, the food is often placed on a plate in the steamer and served directly from it.

Whisk: A whisk about 25 cm (10 in) long and consisting of thin strips of bamboo tied together at the top is used for cleaning a wok.

Wire baskets: Bamboo-handled wire baskets are used to quickly and easily plunge noodles into boiling water for the requisite short cooking time before speedily lifting them out. A Far Eastern kitchen will usually have a set of baskets, as different ones are used for different types of noodles.

Wok: The wok is the cornerstone of Far Eastern cooking and is used for frying, stir-frying, deep-frying and steaming food. Woks come in many sizes; a useful size to buy is about 30-35 cm (12-14 in) in diameter across the top. Choose one that has good deep sides and some weight. Carbon steel is preferable to light stainless steel or aluminium as these tend to develop hot spots which cause sticking, and do not withstand intense heat so well. Non-stick woks and electric ones do not reach sufficiently high temperatures. A metal ring or stand is often used to hold a round-bottomed wok steady over the heat.

CUTTING AND SLICING TECHNIQUES

Although stir-frying is quick and easy, preparation of ingredients is very important and every one must be prepared before cooking begins. Cutting and slicing Far-Eastern style is an art. The size and shape of ingredients determines cooking time, and there is little time for foods to absorb flavours and seasoning. Therefore, cut vegetables thinly, with as many cut surfaces as possible. Cut meats, fish and poultry generally across the grain, for maximum tenderness.

Slicing: Hold food firmly against a cutting board with one hand and, with a knife, slice the food straight down into thin strips. Hold a cleaver with your index finger extended over the top edge and your thumb on the near side, to guide the cutting edge. Hold the food with the other hand, tucking your fingers under, so the blade rests against your knuckles for safety. For matchstick-thin strips, square off the sides of the prepared vegetable, cut crossways into 5 cm (2 in) lengths. Stack a few slices and cut even lengthwise strips.

Shredding: Foods such as cabbage or spinach are easily shredded by piling up a few leaves and cutting lengthwise into thin fine shreds. Roll large leaves, swiss-roll fashion, before cutting, to reduce width. Meat and poultry breasts or cutlets are easier to shred if frozen for about 20 minutes.

Horizontal slicing: To cut thick foods into two or more thin pieces to be sliced or shredded, hold the cleaver or knife parallel to the cutting board. Place one hand flat on the food surface and press down while slicing horizontally into the food. Repeat if necessary.

Diagonal slicing: Most 'long' vegetables, such as spring onions, asparagus or courgettes look attractive and more surface area is exposed for quicker cooking if sliced on the diagonal. Angle the cleaver or knife and cut.

Roll cutting: This is like diagonal cutting, but is suitable for larger or tougher, long vegetables, such as celery or large carrots. Make a diagonal slice at one end, then turn the

vegetable 180° and make another diagonal slice. Continue until the whole vegetable is cut into triangular pieces about 2.5 cm (1 in) long.

Dicing: Cut food into slices, then into lengthwise sticks. Stack the sticks and cut crosswise into even-sized cubes.

Chopping: First cut the food into long strips, align them and, holding them with one hand, fingers tucked under, cut crosswise with a knife or cleaver. Use a rocking motion, keeping the tip of the knife or cleaver against the board and using the knuckles as a guide.

SEASONING AND CLEANING THE WOK

Authentic carbon steel woks must be scrubbed to remove the protective coating of machine oil applied during manufacturing and seasoned before use. To remove this sometimes thick, sticky oil, scrub the wok vigorously with kitchen cleanser and hot water. This is the only time you should scrub the wok, unless it rusts during storage. Dry the wok and place it over a low heat for a few minutes to dry

thoroughly. To season, add 2 tablespoons vegetable oil and, using a double thickness of folded absorbent kitchen paper, rub a thin film of oil all over the inside of the wok. Heat the wok for a few more minutes and wipe again. The paper will probably be black from machine oil residue. Repeat until the paper stays clean. The wok is now ready for use.

Food rarely sticks to a seasoned wok, so an ordinary wash in hot water with no detergent should suffice. If any food has stuck, use a bamboo wok brush, or ordinary plastic kitchen scrubber. Dry the wok thoroughly and put it over a low heat to prevent rust during storage. As a precaution, rub the inside surface of the dry wok with 1 teaspoon of oil. If the wok rusts, repeat the seasoning process.

COOKING TECHNIQUES

Stir-frying: Probably the most important technique in stir-frying is preheating the wok. This prevents food sticking and absorbing excess oil. Place the wok over a moderate heat and wait a few minutes until the wok is very hot. Then add the oil and swirl

to quickly coat the bottom and sides.

For recipes that begin by adding the flavouring ingredients, such as garlic, ginger and spring onions, to the oil, it should be only moderately hot or these delicate ingredients may burn or become bitter. If, however, the first ingredient added is a meat or hearty vegetable, make the oil very hot, just below smoking point. As other ingredients are added, stir-fry over a high heat by stirring and tossing them with the metal spatula or spoon. Allow meat to rest a minute on one side before stirring, to cook and brown. Keep the food moving from the centre, up and out onto the side. If a sauce to be thickened with cornflour is added to the dish, remove the wok briefly from the heat and push the food away from the centre so the sauce-thickening mixture goes directly to the bottom of the wok; stir vigorously and then continue tossing the ingredients in the sauce.

Deep frying: Deep-frying in a wok uses less oil. Foods are often marinated first in soy sauce and spices, then sometimes coated in batter; a mixture of cornflour and egg white is the most usual in Chinese cuisine. Often, food is fried until almost cooked, then removed from the oil. The oil is reheated and the food added again to finish cooking and become really crisp.

Steaming: Steaming is far more popular in the Far East than in the West and is used to cook meat, poultry, fish, dim sum, other pastries and desserts. It was developed as a fuel-saving measure as several foods can be cooked at once in baskets, which are often made of bamboo, stacked above each other. Foods that require the most cooking are put to cook first, and those needing less time are placed on top in succession, as the cooking proceeds.

Red cooking: Food, usually in large pieces, is cooked slowly in dark soy sauce, sometimes with other flavourings added. During the lengthy cooking, which may be as long as 4 hours, the soy imparts a fairly dark, reddish brown colour and a rich flavour to the food. Because of the large amount of soy sauce that is used, the food can also be salty, so sugar may be added to counteract it.

SPRING ONION BRUSHES

4 spring onions (scallions)

Trim away some of green part of spring onion (scallion). Cut off white bulb where it starts to turn green.

Using a small pair of kitchen scissors, make a cut from greenest end of spring onion (scallion), about halfway along the length. Continue to cut onion into fine strips.

Place spring onion (scallion) into a bowl of chilled water. Leave for a few seconds for strips to curl; lift from water several times to ensure they do not curl too tightly. Repeat with remaining spring onions (scallions). Place on absorbent kitchen paper to dry before using.

Makes 4.

CHILLI FLOWERS

4 small fresh chillies

Cut off top of chilli. Insert scissors in hole and cut through chilli flesh almost to stalk end. Give chilli a quarter turn, make another similar cut then repeat twice more.

Remove and discard seeds. Cut through each 'petal' once or twice more to make finer 'petals'.

Place in a bowl of chilled water. Leave for 5-10 minutes for the 'petals' to open into a flower shape. Repeat with remaining chillies. Place on absorbent kitchen paper to dry before using.

Makes 4.

BANANA LEAF CUPS

8 pieces banana leaf, each about 12 cm (5 in) square

Place 2 pieces of banana leaf with dull sides facing each other. Invert a 10 cm (4 in) diameter bowl on top of leaves. Cut around bowl.

Form a 1 cm (½ in) pleat about 4 cm (1½ in) deep in the edge of banana leaf circle. Staple together.

Make an identical pleat in the opposite side of circle, then repeat twice more at points equidistant between the 2 pleats, to make a slightly opened, squared-off cup. Repeat with remaining pieces of banana leaf.

Makes 4 cups.

CARROT FLOWERS

1 young, tender carrot, thinly peeled

Hold carrot pointed end down. Using a small, sharp knife make a cut towards the point to form a petal-shape. Take care not to slice all the way through. Repeat cuts around carrot to make a flower with 4 petals.

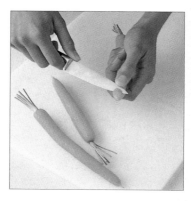

Angle knife slightly, then apply light pressure to separate carrot flower from carrot. For first few flowers it may be necessary to ease every petal in this way, but with a little practice flowers will come away easily with a twist of knife.

Repeat along length of carrot. Arrange flowers singly or group them into clusters.

Note: To improve colour, drop flowers in boiling water, leave 1 minute then drain and rinse under cold running water. Dry well.

PASTES, SAUCES & DIPS

GREEN CURRY PASTE

2 teaspoons coriander seeds
1 teaspoon cumin seeds
1 teaspoon black peppercorns
8 fresh green chillies, seeded and chopped
3 shallots, chopped
4 cloves garlic, crushed
3 coriander roots, chopped
2.5 cm (1 in) piece galangal, chopped
2 stalks lemon grass, chopped
2 kaffir lime leaves, chopped
2 teaspoons shrimp paste
2 tablespoons chopped coriander leaves

Heat a wok, add coriander and cumin seeds
and heat until aroma rises.

Using a pestle and mortar or small blender,
crush coriander and cumin seeds with peppercorns.

Add remaining ingredients and pound or mix
to a smooth paste. Store in an airtight jar in
the refrigerator for up to 4 weeks.

Makes about 8 tablespoons.

Note: The yield and hotness will vary according to the size and heat of the chillies.

RED CURRY PASTE

1 tablespoon coriander seeds
1 teaspoon cumin seeds
1 teaspoon black peppercorns
4 cloves garlic, chopped
3 coriander roots, chopped
8 dried red chillies, seeded and chopped
2 stalks lemon grass, chopped
grated peel ½ kaffir lime
3 cm (1¼ in) piece galangal, chopped
2 teaspoons shrimp paste

Heat a wok, add coriander and cumin seeds
and heat until aroma rises. Using a pestle and
mortar or small blender, crush coriander and
cumin seeds with peppercorns.

Add remaining ingredients and pound or mix
to a smooth paste. Store in an airtight jar in
the refrigerator for up to 4 weeks.

Makes about 4 tablespoons.

Note: The yield and hotness will vary according to the size and heat of the chillies.

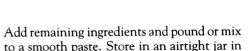

FRAGRANT CURRY PASTE

NAM PRIK

2 cloves garlic, chopped
1 shallot, chopped
4 dried red chillies, seeded and chopped
1 thick stalk lemon grass, chopped
3 coriander roots, chopped
finely grated peel 2 kaffir limes
1 kaffir lime leaf, torn
4 black peppercorns, cracked
½ teaspoon shrimp paste

1 tablespoon fish sauce
about 22 whole dried shrimps, chopped
3 cloves garlic, chopped
4 dried red chillies with seeds, chopped
2 tablespoons lime juice
1 fresh red or green chilli, seeded and chopped
about 1 tablespoon pea aubergines (pea eggplants), if
    desired, chopped

Using a pestle and mortar or small blender,
pound or mix fish sauce, shrimps, garlic,
dried chillies and lime juice to a paste.

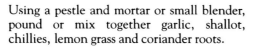

Using a pestle and mortar or small blender,
pound or mix together garlic, shallot,
chillies, lemon grass and coriander roots.

Stir in fresh red or green chilli and pea
aubergines (pea eggplants), if desired.
Transfer paste to a small bowl.

Add lime peel, lime leaf, peppercorns
and shrimp paste, and pound or mix to a
smooth paste. Store in an airtight jar in the
refrigerator for up to 4 weeks.

Makes about 4 tablespoons.

Serve with a selection of raw vegetables.
Store in a covered jar in the refrigerator for
several weeks.

Serves 6-8.

DIPPING SAUCE 1

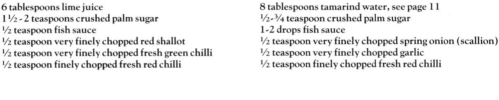

6 tablespoons lime juice
1 1/2 - 2 teaspoons crushed palm sugar
1/2 teaspoon fish sauce
1/2 teaspoon very finely chopped red shallot
1/2 teaspoon very finely chopped fresh green chilli
1/2 teaspoon finely chopped fresh red chilli

In a small bowl, stir together lime juice and sugar until sugar has dissolved. Adjust amount of sugar, if desired.

Stir in fish sauce, shallot and chillies. Pour into a small serving bowl. Serve with deep-fried fish, fish fritters, won tons or spring rolls.

Serves 4.

DIPPING SAUCE 2

8 tablespoons tamarind water, see page 11
1/2-3/4 teaspoon crushed palm sugar
1-2 drops fish sauce
1/2 teaspoon very finely chopped spring onion (scallion)
1/2 teaspoon very finely chopped garlic
1/2 teaspoon finely chopped fresh red chilli

In a small saucepan, gently heat tamarind water and sugar until sugar has dissolved.

Remove pan from heat and add fish sauce. Stir in spring onion (scallion), garlic and chilli. Pour into a small serving bowl and leave to cool.

Serves 4.

SOUPS

CHINESE CHICKEN STOCK

½ chicken
1 bacon hock, split
4 slices root ginger
4 spring onions (scallions), chopped
1 tablespoon chopped parsley
2 litres (64 fl oz/8 cups) fresh water

Place all ingredients in a large saucepan and bring to the boil. Skim. Reduce heat so liquid simmers, cover gently and cook for 3 hours.

Pour into a sieve lined with muslin, placed over a large bowl. Leave to cool completely. Store, covered, in the refrigerator, or freeze in convenient quantities.

Makes 1.75 litres (58 fl oz/7 cups).

Note: Chinese cooks use Chicken Stock for fish dishes (they do not make fish stock). If fish stock is preferred, substitute a favourite recipe.

MUSHROOM SOUP

24 dried black winter mushrooms, soaked in hot water
  25 minutes, drained
1 cm (½ in) piece fresh root ginger, peeled and cut into
  6 slices
2 spring onions (scallions), finely chopped
1½ teaspoons sea salt
1.5 litres (48 fl oz/6 cups) Chinese Chicken Stock
2 teaspoons rice wine or dry sherry
1 teaspoon brown sugar
parsley to garnish

Trim the mushrooms and place in a small saucepan with half the ginger and half the spring onions (scallions). Add ½ teaspoon salt and cover with cold water. Bring slowly to the boil, then simmer for 3 minutes.

Drain. Pour stock into a medium saucepan, add mushrooms and remaining ingredients. Bring slowly to the boil, cover, and simmer gently for 30-35 minutes. Serve hot garnished with parsley.

Serves 4.

HOT AND SOUR SOUP

LEMON GRASS SOUP

4 dried black winter mushrooms, soaked in hot water
   for 25 minutes
85 g (3 oz) Szechuan preserved vegetables, finely sliced
85 g (3 oz) Chinese pickled green vegetables, finely
   sliced
3 spring onions (scallions), finely chopped
3 slices fresh root ginger
850 ml (26 fl oz/3¼ cups) water
1½ teaspoons rice wine or dry sherry
1 tablespoon light soy sauce
2 cakes tofu, finely sliced
1 teaspoon cornflour (cornstarch) dissolved in 2
   teaspoons of water
1 teaspoon sesame oil

175-225 g (6-8 oz) raw large prawns
2 teaspoons vegetable oil
625 ml (20 fl oz/2½ cups) light fish stock
2 thick stalks lemon grass, finely chopped
3 tablespoons lime juice
1 tablespoon fish sauce
3 kaffir lime leaves, chopped
½ fresh red chilli, seeded and thinly sliced
½ fresh green chilli, seeded and thinly sliced
½ teaspoon crushed palm sugar
coriander leaves, to garnish

Peel prawns and remove dark veins running
down their backs; reserve prawns.

Drain mushrooms, discard stalks, squeeze out
all the liquid, then slice very finely. In a
medium saucepan, bring all the ingredients
except cornflour (cornstarch) mixture and
sesame oil to the boil; cook for 3 minutes.

In a wok, heat oil, add prawn shells and fry,
stirring occasionally, until they change
colour. Stir in stock, bring to boil and simmer
for 20 minutes. Strain stock and return to
wok; discard shells. Add lemon grass, lime
juice, fish sauce, lime leaves, chillies and
sugar. Simmer for 2 minutes.

Stir in cornflour (cornstarch) mixture, simmer, still stirring, until thickened, then add
sesame oil.

Serves 4.

Add prawns and cook just below simmering
point for 2-3 minutes until prawns are
cooked. Serve in warmed bowls garnished
with coriander.

Serves 4.

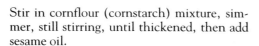

VERMICELLI SOUP

1.1 litres (2 pints/5 cups) chicken stock
1 small onion, chopped
2 stalks lemon grass, chopped and crushed
2 kaffir lime leaves, shredded
1 tablespoon lime juice
3 cloves garlic, chopped
2 fresh red chillies, seeded and chopped
4 cm (1½ in) piece galangal, peeled and chopped
1½ tablespoons fish sauce
2 teaspoons crushed palm sugar
115 g (4 oz) clear vermicelli, soaked in cold water for
    10 minutes, drained
2 tablespoons roughly chopped coriander leaves
Thai holy basil leaves, to garnish

Put stock, onion, lemon grass, lime leaves, lime juice, garlic, chillies and galangal into a saucepan and simmer for 20 minutes.

Stir in fish sauce and sugar. When sugar has dissolved, add noodles and cook for 1 minute. Stir in coriander. Spoon into warmed bowls and garnish with basil leaves.

Serves 4-6.

CHICKEN & ASPARAGUS SOUP

500 ml (16 fl oz/2 cups) Chinese Chicken Stock,
    see page 22
350 g (12 oz) cooked chicken breast meat, finely sliced
2 teaspoons cornflour (cornstarch) dissolved in
    1 tablespoon water
12 button mushrooms, sliced
85 g (3 oz) canned asparagus tips, drained and chopped
85 g (3 oz) canned sweetcorn, drained
1½ teaspoons sea salt
1 teaspoon sesame oil to serve
2 spring onions (scallions), finely chopped to garnish

In a saucepan bring chicken stock to the boil. Add the chicken, simmer for 2-3 minutes, then stir in cornflour (cornstarch) mixture and simmer, still stirring, until thickened.

Reduce heat, add mushrooms, asparagus and sweetcorn and heat through gently but thoroughly. Season with salt. Serve sprinkled with sesame oil and garnished with chopped spring onions (scallions).

Serves 4.

MEATBALL SOUP

CHICKEN & MUSHROOM SOUP

500 g (1 lb) pork tenderloin, finely minced
3 dried black winter mushrooms, soaked in hot water
    for 25 minutes, drained and finely chopped
2 spring onions (scallions), very finely chopped
2 tablespoons light soy sauce
sea salt
85 g (3 oz/⅔ cup) cornflour (cornstarch) for coating
½ teaspoon ground black pepper
3 tablespoons peanut oil
2 litres (64 fl oz/8 cups) Chinese Chicken Stock, see
    page 22
chopped parsley to garnish

2 cloves garlic, crushed
4 coriander sprigs
1½ teaspoons black peppercorns, crushed
1 tablespoon vegetable oil
1 litre (35 fl oz/4¼ cups) chicken stock
5 pieces dried Chinese black mushrooms, soaked in
    cold water for 20 minutes, drained and coarsely
    chopped
1 tablespoon fish sauce
115 g (4 oz) chicken, cut into strips
55 g (2 oz) spring onions (scallions), thinly sliced
coriander sprigs, to garnish

In a bowl, mix together pork, mushrooms, spring onions (scallions), soy sauce and 1 teaspoon salt. Pass through the finest blade on a mincer. Roll mixture into 2.5 cm (1 in) balls. Roll balls in cornflour (cornstarch) to lightly coat.

Using a pestle and mortar or small blender, pound or mix garlic, coriander stalks and leaves and peppercorns to a paste. In a wok, heat oil, add paste and cook, stirring, for 1 minute. Stir in stock, mushrooms and fish sauce. Simmer for 5 minutes.

In a wok, heat oil and fry the balls for about 4 minutes until lightly and evenly browned. Drain on absorbent kitchen paper. In a saucepan, heat chicken stock to the boil. Reduce heat so stock simmers, then add meatballs. Season with salt and pepper. Garnish with chopped parsley.

Serves 4.

Add chicken, lower heat so liquid barely moves and cook gently for 5 minutes. Scatter spring onions (scallions) over surface and garnish with coriander sprigs.

Serves 4.

PORK & PEANUT SOUP

4 coriander roots, chopped
2 cloves garlic, chopped
1 teaspoon black peppercorns, cracked
1 tablespoon vegetable oil
225 g (8 oz) lean pork, finely chopped
4 spring onions (scallions), chopped
700 ml (24 fl oz/3 cups) veal stock
55 g (2 oz) skinned peanuts
6 pieces dried Chinese black mushrooms, soaked for
    20 minutes, drained and chopped
115 g (4 oz) bamboo shoots, roughly chopped
1 tablespoon fish sauce

Using a pestle and mortar, pound coriander, garlic and peppercorns to a paste.

In a wok, heat oil, add peppercorn paste and cook for 2-3 minutes, stirring occasionally. Add pork and spring onions (scallions) and stir for 1½ minutes.

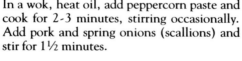

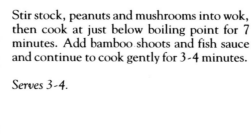

Stir stock, peanuts and mushrooms into wok, then cook at just below boiling point for 7 minutes. Add bamboo shoots and fish sauce and continue to cook gently for 3-4 minutes.

Serves 3-4.

CHICKEN & COCONUT SOUP

950 ml (30 fl oz/3¾ cups) coconut milk
115 g (4 oz) chicken breast meat, cut into strips
2 stalks lemon grass, bruised and thickly sliced
2 spring onions (scallions), thinly sliced
3-4 fresh red chillies, seeded and sliced
juice 1½ limes
1 tablespoon fish sauce
1 tablespoon coriander leaves, freshly torn into shreds
coriander leaves, to garnish

Bring coconut milk to just below boiling point in a saucepan. Add chicken and lemon grass.

Adjust heat so liquid gives just an occasional bubble, then poach chicken, uncovered, for about 4 minutes until tender.

Add spring onions (scallions) and chillies. Heat briefly, then remove from heat and stir in lime juice, fish sauce and shredded coriander. Serve garnished with coriander leaves.

Serves 4.

STARTERS & SNACKS

PRAWN TOASTS

30 g (1 oz) pork fat, finely minced
175 g (6 oz) peeled prawns, finely minced
¼ teaspoon sea salt
1 tablespoon cornflour (cornstarch)
1 egg white, lightly beaten
white pepper
3 thin slices white bread, crusts removed
115 g (4 oz) sesame seeds
625 ml (20 fl oz/2½ cups) vegetable oil

In a bowl, mix together fat, prawns, salt,
cornflour (cornstarch) and egg white. Season
with white pepper.

Spread prawn mixture on to one side of each
slice of bread.

Coat with a thick layer of sesame seeds, and
press well into the spread. Cut each slice into
4 triangles. In a wok, heat oil until smoking,
reduce heat slightly, then carefully lower in
the triangles, coated side down. Deep-fry for
2-3 minutes until golden brown. Drain on
absorbent kitchen paper. Serve hot.

Serves 4.

SPRING ROLLS

20 spring roll skins
1 litre (35 fl oz/4 cups) vegetable oil
FILLING:
3 tablespoons peanut oil
225 g (8 oz) bean sprouts
6 spring onions (scallions), thinly shredded
115 g (4 oz) carrots, cut into thin sticks
115 g (4 oz) button mushrooms, thinly sliced
1 clove garlic, very finely chopped
¼ teaspoon five-spice powder
1 tablespoon light soy sauce
1 teaspoon sea salt

To make the filling, heat peanut oil in a wok
and stir-fry vegetables, garlic and tofu for
about 1 minute. Add five-spice powder, soy
sauce and salt and continue stir-frying for 2
minutes. Allow to cool. To fill the skins, lay
one flat on a work surface. Place a portion of
filling slightly off-centre. Fold the sides of the
skin neatly over the filling, then roll up to
enclose the filling completely. Brush around
the edges with beaten egg to seal.

In a wok or deep-fat frying pan, heat vegetable oil until smoking. Reduce heat slightly,
add 4 spring rolls and fry for 4 minutes, until
crisp and golden. Drain on absorbent kitchen
paper. Keep warm. Re-heat oil, reduce heat
and cook 4 more spring rolls. Repeat with
remaining rolls.

Variations: Use 175 g (6 oz) chopped, prepared prawns, see page 14, in place of the
tofu.

Serves 4.

PORK DIM SUM

350 g (12 oz) minced pork
115 g (4 oz) raw shelled prawns, ground
1½ tablespoons soy sauce
½ tablespoon rice wine or dry sherry
½ tablespoon sesame oil
½ tablespoon sugar
dash of pepper
1 egg white
1½ tablespoons cornflour (cornstarch)
30 won ton skins
fresh or frozen green peas or chopped hard-cooked egg
     yolks, for garnish

To make filling: Mix together ground pork, ground prawns, soy sauce, rice wine or dry sherry, sesame oil, sugar, pepper and egg white until mixture is well blended and smooth. Stir in cornflour. Divide into 30 portions. Cut off the edges of won ton skins to form circles, if necessary. Place 1 portion of filling in the middle of a won ton skin. Gather the edges of the won ton skin around the meat filling. Dip a teaspoon in water and use to smooth the surface of the meat.

Garnish by placing a green pea or chopped egg yolk on top of meat. Gather the edges to form a waist. Repeat with remaining won ton skins and meat filling. Line a steamer with a damp cloth; steam over high heat 5 minutes. Remove and serve.

Makes 30 dumplings.

PRAWN DIM SUM

350 g (12 oz) raw shelled prawns, ground
115 g (4 oz) can bamboo shoots, chopped
4 tablespoons water
1½ tablespoons soy sauce
½ tablespoon rice wine or dry sherry
½ teaspoon sugar
½ teaspoon sesame oil
dash of pepper
1½ tablespoons cornflour (cornstarch)
DOUGH:
350 g (12 oz/2½ cups) plain (all-purpose) flour
115 ml (4 fl oz/½ cup) boiling water
70 ml (2½ fl oz/⅓ cup) cold water
1 tablespoon vegetable oil

To make filling: Mix together all ingredients except cornflour until the mixture is well blended and smooth. Stir in cornflour. Divide into 30 portions.

To make dough: Put 315 g (10 fl oz/2 cups) of flour in a medium size bowl. Reserve remainder and use for hands if they become sticky. Stir in boiling water. Add cold water and oil. Mix to form dough; knead until smooth. Roll dough into a long, rope shape and cut it into 30 pieces. Use a rolling pin to roll each portion into a thin 5 cm (2 in) circle.

Place 1 portion of the filling in the middle of a dough circle. Bring the opposite edges together and pinch them together to hold. Repeat with remaining circles and filling. Line a steamer with a damp cloth. Set the dim sum about 2.5 cm (1 in) apart. Steam over high heat 5 minutes. Remove and serve.

Makes 30 dumplings.

GOLD BAGS

SWEETCORN CAKES

115 g (4 oz) cooked peeled prawns, finely chopped
55 g (2 oz) canned water chestnuts, finely chopped
2 spring onions (scallions), white part only, finely
   chopped
1 teaspoon fish sauce
freshly ground black pepper
16 won ton skins
vegetable oil for deep frying
Dipping Sauce 2, see page 20
coriander sprig, to garnish

In a bowl, mix together prawns, water chestnuts, spring onions (scallions), fish sauce and
black pepper.

350 g (12 oz) sweetcorn kernels
1 tablespoon Green Curry Paste, see page 18
2 tablespoons plain flour
3 tablespoons rice flour
3 spring onions (scallions), finely chopped
1 egg, beaten
2 teaspoons fish sauce
vegetable oil for deep frying
2.5 cm (1 in) piece of cucumber
Dipping Sauce 1, see page 20
1 tablespoon ground roasted peanuts

To shape each bag, put a small amount of
prawn mixture in centre of each won ton
skin. Dampen edges of skins with a little
water, then bring up over filling to form a
'dolly bag'. Press edges together to seal.

Place sweetcorn in a blender, add curry paste,
plain flour, rice flour, spring onions (scallions), egg and fish sauce and mix together so
corn is slightly broken up. Form into about 16
cakes. Heat oil in a wok to 180C (350F),
then deep fry one batch of sweetcorn cakes
for about 3 minutes until golden brown.

In a wok, heat oil to 190C (375F). Add bags
in batches and fry for about 2-3 minutes until
crisp and golden. Using a slotted spoon,
transfer to absorbent kitchen paper to drain.
Serve hot with dipping sauce. Garnish with
coriander sprig.

Makes 16.

Using a slotted spoon, transfer to absorbent
kitchen paper to drain. Keep warm while
frying remaining cakes. Peel cucumber,
quarter lengthwise, remove seeds, then slice
thinly. Place in a small bowl and mix in
dipping sauce and ground peanuts. Serve
with warm sweetcorn cakes.

Makes about 16.

EGG NESTS

1 tablespoon chopped coriander roots
1 clove garlic, chopped
½ teaspoon black peppercorns, cracked
1 tablespoon peanut oil
½ small onion, finely chopped
115 g (4 oz) lean pork, very finely chopped
115 g (4 oz) raw peeled prawns, chopped
2 teaspoons fish sauce
3 tablespoons vegetable oil
2 eggs
3 fresh red chillies, seeded and cut into fine strips
20-30 coriander leaves
coriander sprigs, to garnish

Add vegetable oil to wok and place over medium heat. In a small bowl, beat eggs. Spoon egg into a cone of greaseproof paper with a very small hole in pointed end. Move cone above surface of pan, so trail of egg flows onto it and sets in threads. Quickly repeat, moving in another direction directly over threads. Repeat until there are 4 crisscrossing layers of egg.

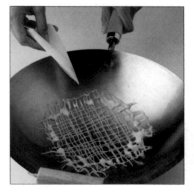

Using a pestle and mortar, pound together coriander roots, garlic and peppercorns. In a wok, heat peanut oil, add peppercorn mixture and onion and stir-fry for 1 minute.

Using a spatula, transfer nest to absorbent kitchen paper. Repeat with remaining egg to make more nests. Place nests with flat side facing downwards. Place 2 strips of chilli to form a cross on each nest.

Add pork, stir-fry for 1 minute, then stir in prawns for 45 seconds. Quickly stir in fish sauce, then transfer mixture to a bowl. Using absorbent kitchen paper, wipe out wok.

Top with coriander leaves, then about 1 tablespoon of pork mixture. Fold nests over filling, turn over and arrange on serving plate. Garnish with coriander sprigs.

Serves 4.

STEAMED CRAB

STUFFED OMELETTE

1 clove garlic, chopped
1 small shallot, chopped
6 coriander sprigs, stalks finely chopped
175 g (6 oz) cooked crab meat
115 g (4 oz) lean pork, very finely chopped and cooked
1 egg, beaten
1 tablespoon coconut cream, see page 10
2 teaspoons fish sauce
freshly ground black pepper
1 fresh chilli, seeded and cut into fine strips

2½ tablespoons vegetable oil
1 small onion, quartered and thinly sliced
3 cloves garlic, chopped
8 coriander roots, chopped
14 black peppercorns, cracked
150 g (5 oz) lean pork, very finely chopped
150 g (5 oz) long beans, or green beans, thinly sliced
    and cut into 3 cm (1¼ in) lengths
8 eggs, beaten
2 teaspoons fish sauce
4 tablespoons chopped coriander leaves
coriander sprigs, to garnish

In a wok, heat 2 tablespoons oil, add onion and cook, stirring until lightly browned.

Using a pestle and mortar, pound garlic, shallot and coriander stalks to a paste. In a bowl, stir together crab meat, pork, garlic paste, egg, coconut cream, fish sauce and plenty of black pepper until evenly mixed.

Using a pestle and mortar or small blender, pound or mix together garlic, coriander roots and peppercorns. Stir into wok and cook, stirring occasionally, for 2 minutes. Add pork, stir-fry for 2 minutes, then stir in beans. Stir-fry for 2 minutes. Cover wok and set aside.

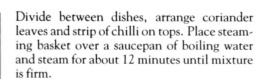

Divide between dishes, arrange coriander leaves and strip of chilli on tops. Place steaming basket over a saucepan of boiling water and steam for about 12 minutes until mixture is firm.

Serves 4.

Note: Crab shells may be used instead of dishes for cooking.

In a small bowl, mix eggs with fish sauce and coriander. In a frying pan, heat remaining oil, pour in half of egg mixture and tilt pan to form a thin, even layer. Cook briefly until lightly set. Spoon half of reserved filling down the centre. Fold sides over filling to form a square package, then slide onto a warmed plate. Keep warm while making second omelette with remaining egg and filling. Garnish with coriander sprigs.

Serves 4-6.

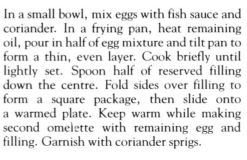

STUFFED CHICKEN WINGS

4 large chicken wings
lean pork, finely minced, (see method)
55 g (2 oz) cooked peeled prawns, chopped
3 spring onions (scallions), finely chopped
2 large cloves garlic, chopped
3 coriander roots, chopped
2 tablespoons fish sauce
freshly ground black pepper
vegetable oil for deep frying
rice flour for coating
Dipping Sauce 1, see page 20, to serve
lettuce leaves, to garnish

Chop chicken flesh from wings. Make up to 175 g (6 oz) with pork, if necessary. Place chicken and pork, if used, in a bowl and thoroughly mix together with prawns and spring onions (scallions). Divide between chicken wings; set aside.

Bend wing joints backwards against joint. Using a small sharp knife or kitchen scissors, cut around top of bone that attaches wing to chicken body. Using blade of knife, scrape meat and skin down length of first bone, turning skin back over unboned portion. Break bone free at joint.

Using a pestle and mortar, pound together garlic and coriander roots. Stir in fish sauce and plenty of black pepper. Pour over chicken wings, stirring them to coat with mixture, then set aside for 30 minutes.

Ease skin over joint and detach from flesh and bone. Working down next adjacent bones, scrape off flesh and skin taking care not to puncture skin. Break bones free at joint, leaving end section.

Heat oil in a wok to 180C (350F). Remove chicken wings from bowl, then toss in rice flour to coat completely. Add 2 at a time to oil and deep fry for about 3-4 minutes until browned. Using a slotted spoon, transfer to absorbent kitchen paper to drain. Keep warm while frying remaining 2 chicken wings. Serve with sauce and garnish with lettuce leaves.

Serves 4.

PORK TOASTS

175 g (6 oz) lean pork, minced
55 g (2 oz) cooked peeled prawns, finely chopped
2 cloves garlic, finely chopped
1 tablespoon chopped coriander leaves
1½ spring onions (scallions), finely chopped
2 eggs, beaten
2 teaspoons fish sauce
freshly ground black pepper
4 day-old slices of bread
1 tablespoon coconut milk
vegetable oil for deep frying
coriander leaves, fine rings of fresh red chilli and
    cucumber slices, to garnish

In a bowl, mix together pork and prawns using a fork, then thoroughly mix in garlic, coriander, spring onions (scallions), half of egg, the fish sauce and black pepper. Divide between bread, spreading it firmly to edges. In a small bowl, stir together remaining egg and coconut milk and brush over pork mixture. Trim crusts from bread, then cut each slice into squares.

In a wok, heat oil to 190C (375F). Add several squares at a time, pork-side down, and fry for 3-4 minutes until crisp, turning over halfway through. Using a slotted spoon, transfer to absorbent kitchen paper to drain, then keep warm in oven. Check temperature of oil in between frying each batch. Serve warm, garnished with coriander and slices of chilli and cucumber.

Serves 4-6.

PORK & NOODLE PARCELS

3 cloves garlic, chopped
4 coriander roots, chopped
175 g (6 oz) lean pork, minced
1 small egg, beaten
2 teaspoons fish sauce
freshly ground black pepper
about 55 g (2 oz) egg thread noodles (1 'nest')
vegetable oil for deep frying
Dipping Sauce 2, see page 20, to serve
coriander sprig, to garnish

Using a pestle and mortar or small blender, pound or mix together garlic and coriander roots. In a bowl, mix together pork, egg, fish sauce and pepper, then stir in garlic mixture.

Place noodles in a heatproof sieve and dip in boiling water for 5 seconds if fresh, about 2 minutes if dried, until separated. Remove and rinse immediately in cold running water. Form pork mixture into approximately 12 balls. Neatly and evenly wind 3 or 4 strands of noodles around each ball to cover completely.

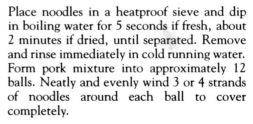

In a wok, heat oil to 180C (350F). Using a slotted spoon, lower 4-6 balls into oil and cook for about 3 minutes until golden and pork is cooked through. Using a slotted or draining spoon, transfer to absorbent kitchen paper to drain. Keep warm while cooking remaining balls. Serve hot with dipping sauce. Garnish with coriander sprig.

Makes about 12 parcels.

FISH & SHELLFISH

PRAWNS WITH GARLIC

JACKETED PRAWNS

2 tablespoons vegetable oil
5 cloves garlic, chopped
0.5 cm (¼ in) slice fresh root ginger, very finely chopped
14-16 large prawns, peeled, tails left on
2 teaspoons fish sauce
2 tablespoons chopped coriander leaves
freshly ground black pepper
lettuce leaves, lime juice and diced cucumber, to serve

In a wok, heat oil, add garlic and fry until browned.

4 cm (1½ in) length cucumber
Dipping Sauce 2, see page 20
8 raw Mediterranean (king) prawns
vegetable oil for deep frying
leaves from 1 coriander sprig, chopped
BATTER:
115 g (4 oz/⅔ cup) rice flour
3 tablespoons desiccated coconut
1 egg, separated
185 ml (6 fl oz/¾ cup) coconut milk
1 teaspoon fish sauce

Stir in ginger, heat for 30 seconds, then add prawns and stir-fry for 2-3 minutes until beginning to turn opaque. Stir in fish sauce, coriander, 1-2 tablespoons water and plenty of black pepper. Allow to bubble for 1-2 minutes.

Cut cucumber into quarters lengthwise, remove and discard seeds, then thickly slice. Place in a small bowl and add dipping sauce. Set aside. Peel prawns, leaving tails on. Cut along back of each one and remove black spinal cord. Set prawns aside. In a wok, heat oil to 180C (350F).

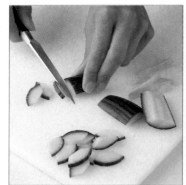

Serve prawns on a bed of lettuce leaves with lime juice squeezed over and scattered with cucumber.

Serves 4.

For batter, in a bowl, stir together flour and coconut. Gradually stir in egg yolk, coconut milk and fish sauce. In a bowl, whisk egg white until stiff; fold into batter. Dip prawns in batter to coat evenly. Deep fry in batches for 2-3 minutes until golden. Using a slotted spoon, transfer to absorbent kitchen paper. Keep warm while frying remainder. Add coriander to sauce and serve with prawns.

Serves 3-4.

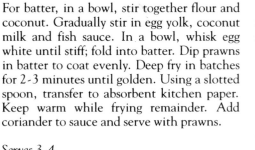

STIR-FRIED PRAWNS & GINGER

—PRAWNS IN COCONUT SAUCE—

3 cloves garlic, crushed
4 cm (1½ in) piece fresh root ginger, thinly sliced
2 tablespoons vegetable oil
12-16 raw Mediterranean (king) prawns, peeled and deveined
2 red shallots, finely chopped
grated peel ½ kaffir lime
2 teaspoons fish sauce
3 spring onions (scallions), thinly sliced
lime juice, to serve
Spring Onion (Scallion) Brushes, see page 15, to garnish

2 fresh red chillies, seeded and chopped
1 red onion, chopped
1 thick stalk lemon grass, chopped
2.5 cm (1 in) piece galangal, chopped
1 teaspoon ground turmeric
250 ml (8 fl oz/1 cup) coconut milk
14-16 raw Mediterranean (king) prawns, peeled and deveined
8 Thai holy basil leaves
2 teaspoons lime juice
1 teaspoon fish sauce
1 spring onion (scallion), including some green, cut into fine strips

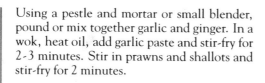

Using a pestle and mortar or small blender, pound or mix together garlic and ginger. In a wok, heat oil, add garlic paste and stir-fry for 2-3 minutes. Stir in prawns and shallots and stir-fry for 2 minutes.

Using a small blender, mix chillies, onion, lemon grass and galangal to a paste. Transfer to a wok and heat, stirring, for 2-3 minutes. Stir in turmeric and 125 ml (4 fl oz/½ cup) water, bring to the boil and simmer for 3-4 minutes until most of the water has evaporated.

Stir in lime peel, fish sauce and 3 tablespoons water. Allow to bubble for 1 minute until prawns become opaque and cooked through. Stir in spring onions (scallions), then remove from heat. Serve in a warmed dish, sprinkled with lime juice and garnished with spring onion (scallion) brushes.

Serves 3-4.

Stir in coconut milk and prawns and cook gently, stirring occasionally, for about 4 minutes until prawns are just firm and pink. Stir in basil leaves, lime juice and fish sauce. Scatter over strips of spring onion (scallion).

Serves 4.

KUNG PO PRAWNS

SZECHUAN PRAWNS

500 g (1 lb) prepared raw prawns
5-6 tablespoons water
4 tablespoons cornflour (cornstarch)
625 ml (20 fl oz/2½ cups) peanut oil
2 spring onions (scallions), finely chopped
1 cm (½ in) piece fresh root ginger, peeled and finely
   chopped
1 tablespoon rice wine or dry sherry
1 tablespoon light soy sauce
1 teaspoon brown sugar
2 teaspoons sherry vinegar
sea salt and black pepper

500 g (1 lb) prepared raw prawns
2 tablespoons vegetable oil
1 clove garlic, finely chopped
1 small fresh red chilli, seeded if desired, finely chopped
1½ teaspoons chilli sauce
¼ teaspoon cornflour (cornstarch)
¼ teaspoon sea salt
¼ teaspoon brown sugar
2 tablespoons Chinese Chicken Stock, see page 22

In a bowl, stir water into cornflour (cornstarch) to make a light batter. Dip prawns in batter to coat evenly; allow excess batter to drain off. In a wok, heat oil until smoking, add prawns and deep-fry for about 3 minutes until golden brown. Using a slotted spoon, remove and then drain on absorbent kitchen paper.

Bring a large saucepan of salted water to the boil, add prawns, boil for 1 minute then drain. In a wok, heat oil, garlic and chilli and stir-fry for 30 seconds. Add chilli sauce and stir for 3 minutes.

Pour oil from wok, leaving just 2 tablespoonsful. Add spring onions (scallions) and ginger and stir-fry for 1 minute. Stir in remaining ingredients and bring to the boil. Add prawns to sauce and heat gently until sauce has thickened.

Serves 4.

In a small bowl mix together cornflour (cornstarch), stock, sugar and salt until smooth, then stir into the wok. Bring to the boil, stirring, then simmer until sauce is thick. Add prawns and gently heat through for about 2 minutes.

Serves 4.

—PRAWN & CUCUMBER CURRY—

—JASMINE-SCENTED PRAWNS—

4 tablespoons coconut cream, see page 10
3-4 tablespoons Red Curry Paste, see page 18
225 g (8 oz) raw large peeled prawns
20 cm (8 in) length cucumber, halved lengthwise, seeded and cut into 2 cm (¾ in) pieces
315 ml (10 fl oz/1¼ cups) coconut milk
2 tablespoons tamarind water, see page 12
1 teaspoon crushed palm sugar
coriander leaves, to garnish

3 tablespoons Japanese rice wine, sake or dry sherry
1 tablespoon light soy sauce
2.5 cm (1 in) piece fresh root ginger, peeled and finely chopped
1 teaspoon sesame oil
¼ teaspoon salt
700 g (1½ lb) raw medium prawns, shelled and deveined, tails left on if wished
2 tablespoons jasmine or other aromatic tea leaves, such as Earl Grey
115 ml (4 fl oz/½ cup) light fish or chicken stock
2 teaspoons cornflour, dissolved in 1 tablespoon water
½ teaspoon sugar
1 tablespoon vegetable oil
4 spring onions, thinly sliced
mint sprigs or jasmine flowers, to garnish

In a wok, heat coconut cream, stirring, until it boils, thickens and oil begins to form. Add curry paste. Stir in prawns to coat, then stir in cucumber. Add coconut milk, tamarind water and sugar.

In a medium bowl, combine rice wine, sake or dry sherry, soy sauce, ginger, sesame oil and salt. Add prawns and toss to coat well. Allow to stand for 30 minutes, stirring once or twice. In a small bowl, stir the tea leaves into 115 ml (4 fl oz/½ cup) boiling water and allow to steep for 1 minute. Strain tea through a fine tea strainer or sieve into another bowl and discard the tea leaves. Add the fish or chicken stock to the tea and stir in the cornflour mixture and sugar.

Cook gently for about 3-4 minutes until prawns are just cooked through. Transfer to warmed serving dish and garnish with coriander.

Serves 3.

Heat wok until hot, add vegetable oil and swirl to coat wok. With a Chinese strainer or slotted spoon, remove prawns from marinade. Working in batches, add prawns to wok and stir-fry for 1-2 minutes until pink and firm; remove to a bowl. Stir in spring onions and reserved marinade and cook for 1 minute. Stir tea mixture and add to wok, stirring until thickened. Return prawns to wok and toss lightly to coat. Garnish with mint or jasmine and serve with rice.

Serves 4.

MUSSELS WITH BEANS & CHILLI —— MUSSELS WITH BASIL —

3.25 kg (8 lb) mussels, scrubbed and rinsed
125 ml (4 fl oz/½ cup) vegetable oil
4 cloves garlic, finely chopped
2 hot red chillies, finely chopped
½ green pepper (capsicum), chopped
3 spring onions (scallions), sliced
1 teaspoon cornflour (cornstarch) dissolved in
    2 teaspoons water
4 tablespoons rice wine or dry sherry
3 tablespoons black bean paste
2 teaspoons ground ginger
1 tablespoon brown sugar
2 tablespoons hot chilli paste
3 tablespoons oyster sauce
750 ml (24 fl oz/3 cups) Chinese Chicken Stock, see
    page 22

700 g (1½ lb) fresh mussels in shell, cleaned, bearded
    and rinsed
1 large clove garlic, chopped
7.5 cm (3 in) piece galangal, thickly sliced
2 stalks lemon grass, chopped
10 Thai holy basil sprigs
1 tablespoon fish sauce
Thai holy basil leaves, to garnish
Dipping Sauce 1, see page 20, to serve

Place mussels in a large saucepan, add 500 ml
(16 fl oz/2 cups) water, cover and place over a
high flame for about 5 minutes, or until the
mussels have opened, shaking pan occasionally; this may have to be done in batches.
Remove from heat, drain and discard any
mussels which have not opened. In a wok,
heat oil, add garlic, chilli, green pepper
(capsicum) and spring onions (scallions) and
stir-fry for 1 minute.

Place mussels, garlic, galangal, lemon grass,
basil sprigs and fish sauce in a large saucepan.
Add water to a depth of 1 cm (½ in), cover
pan, bring to the boil and cook for about
5 minutes, shaking pan frequently, until
mussels have opened; discard any that remain
closed.

In a bowl stir together remaining ingredients,
stir into wok and bring to the boil, stirring.
Simmer until lightly thickened. Add mussels
to wok and heat through for 5 minutes,
occasionally shaking wok.

Serves 4-6.

Transfer mussels to a large warmed bowl, or
individual bowls, and strain over cooking
liquid. Scatter over basil leaves. Serve with
sauce to dip mussels into.

Serves 2-3.

CLAMS WITH SOY & SESAME DIP

1 kg (2 lb) clams in shells, scrubbed and rinsed
1 teaspoon sea salt
4 spring onions (scallions), finely chopped
3 cm (1½ in) piece fresh root ginger, peeled and finely chopped
4 tablespoons dark soy sauce
1 teaspoon medium sherry
2 tablespoons sesame oil

Bring a large saucepan of salted water to a rapid boil, add clams and boil for 10 minutes until clams have opened. Discard any clams that do not open.

Drain the clams and remove and discard the top shells.

Sprinkle each clam with spring onions (scallions) and ginger. In a bowl mix together the soy sauce, sherry and sesame oil. Spoon a little over each clam.

Serves 4.

-SQUID FLOWERS WITH PEPPERS-

625 ml (20 fl oz/2½ cups) peanut oil
500 g (1 lb) prepared squid
2 slices fresh root ginger, peeled and finely chopped
1 large green pepper (capsicum), seeded and cut into 2.5 cm (1 in) squares
1 teaspoon sea salt
1 tablespoon dark soy sauce
1 teaspoon rice vinegar
½ teaspoon brown sugar
ground black pepper
1 teaspoon sesame oil

In a wok, heat oil until smoking, add squid and fry for 1 minute. Remove and drain on absorbent kitchen paper. Pour oil from wok, leaving just 1 tablespoonful. Add ginger and green pepper (capsicum) and stir-fry for 5 minutes until the pepper (capsicum) begins to soften.

Stir in remaining ingredients except sesame oil, bring to the boil, stirring, reduce heat so sauce is simmering then add squid and gently heat through. Transfer to a warmed serving plate and sprinkle with sesame oil.

Serves 4.

CRAB WONTONS

70 ml (2½ fl oz/⅓ cup) light soy sauce
2 tablespoons wine vinegar
2 tablespoons sesame oil
½ teaspoon crushed dried chillies
2 teaspoons honey or sugar
6-8 canned whole water chestnuts, rinsed and minced
2 spring onions, finely chopped
1 teaspoon finely chopped fresh root ginger
225 g (8 oz) white crabmeat, drained and picked over
½ teaspoon red pepper sauce
1 tablespoon finely chopped fresh coriander or dill
1 egg yolk
30 wonton skins
vegetable oil for deep frying

In a small bowl, mix together 55 ml (2 fl oz/¼ cup) soy sauce, wine vinegar, 1 tablespoon sesame oil, 1 tablespoon water, crushed chillies and honey or sugar. Set aside. Heat remaining oil in the wok, add the water chestnuts, spring onions and root ginger and stir-fry for 1-2 minutes. Cool slightly, then mix with crab, remaining soy sauce, red pepper sauce, fresh coriander or dill and egg yolk. Place a teaspoon of mixture in the centre of each wonton skin. Dampen edges with a little water and fold up one corner to opposite corner to form a triangle.

Fold over the bottom 2 corners to meet and press together to resemble a tortelloni. Be sure the filling is well-sealed. In the wok, heat 7.5 cm (3 in) vegetable oil to 190C (375F) and deep fry the wontons in batches for 3 minutes, until golden on all sides, turning once during cooking. Remove with a Chinese strainer or slotted spoon to absorbent kitchen paper to drain. Serve with the dipping sauce and a salad.

Makes 30 wontons.

DEEP-FRIED CRAB CLAWS

4 large crab claws
315 g (10 oz) prepared raw prawns, minced
½ teaspoon sea salt
pinch of ground white pepper
1 teaspoon cornflour (cornstarch)
1 egg white
115 g (4 oz/1 cup) dried white breadcrumbs to coat
625 ml (20 fl oz/2½ cups) peanut oil

Crack and remove the main shell from each claw, leaving the pincer part intact.

Bring a large saucepan of salted water to the boil. Add crab claws, return to the boil and boil for 1 minute. Drain and refresh under cold running water. In a bowl, mash to an even paste the prawns, salt, pepper, cornflour (cornstarch) and egg white. Divide into 4 portions and press a portion around each claw, leaving pincer showing.

Place breadcrumbs on plate, roll claws in breadcrumbs to evenly coat. In a wok, heat oil, add claws and fry for 10 minutes until golden brown. Drain on absorbent kitchen paper.

Serves 4.

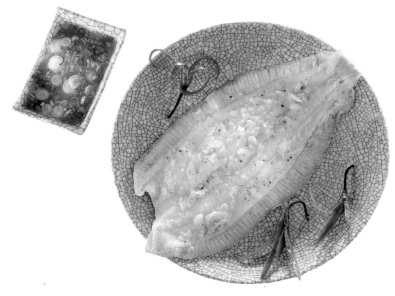

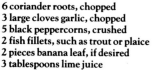

—FISH WITH LEMON GRASS—

2 tablespoons vegetable oil
1 flat fish, such as pomfret, plump lemon sole or plaice,
  gutted and cleaned
4 cloves garlic, finely chopped
2 fresh red chillies, seeded and finely chopped
1 red shallot, chopped
4½ tablespoons lime juice
½ teaspoon crushed palm sugar
1½ tablespoons finely chopped lemon grass
2 teaspoons fish sauce
Chilli Flowers, see page 15, to garnish

In a wok, heat oil, add fish, skin-side down first, and cook for 3-5 minutes a side until lightly browned and lightly cooked. Using a fish slice, transfer to a warmed serving plate, cover and keep warm. Add garlic to wok and fry, stirring occasionally, until browned.

Stir in chillies, shallot, lime juice, sugar, lemon grass and fish sauce. Allow to simmer gently for 1-2 minutes. Pour over fish and garnish with chilli flowers.

Serves 2.

—CORIANDER FISH & GARLIC—

6 coriander roots, chopped
3 large cloves garlic, chopped
5 black peppercorns, crushed
2 fish fillets, such as trout or plaice
2 pieces banana leaf, if desired
3 tablespoons lime juice
½ teaspoon crushed palm sugar
1 spring onion (scallion), finely chopped
½ small fresh green chilli, seeded and thinly sliced
½ small fresh red chilli, seeded and thinly sliced
Chilli flowers, see page 15, to garnish

Using a pestle and mortar or small blender, briefly mix together coriander roots, garlic and peppercorns. Spread evenly over inside of fish fillets; set aside for 30 minutes.

Wrap fish in banana leaves or pieces of foil, securing leaf with wooden cocktail stick (toothpick), or folding edges of foil tightly together. Grill for about 8 minutes. Meanwhile, in a bowl, stir together lime juice and sugar, then stir in spring onion (scallion) and chillies. Serve with fish. Garnish with chilli flowers.

Serves 2.

—FISH IN BANANA LEAF CUPS—

85 g (3 oz) firm white fish, such as cod, hake,
   monkfish, very finely chopped
85 g (3 oz) cooked peeled prawns, very finely chopped
2-3 teaspoons Red Curry Paste, see page 18
2 tablespoons ground peanuts
1 kaffir lime leaf, finely chopped
2 tablespoons coconut milk
1 egg
2 teaspoons fish sauce
leaf part of ½ Chinese cabbage, finely shredded
2 Banana Leaf Cups, see page 16, if desired
2 teaspoons coconut cream, see page 10
strips fresh red chilli, to garnish

In a bowl, work fish and prawns together
using a fork. Mix in curry paste, peanuts and
lime leaf. In a small bowl, mix together coconut milk, egg and fish sauce. Stir into fish
mixture to evenly combine; set aside for 30
minutes.

Divide cabbage leaf between banana cups, or
heatproof individual dishes, to make a fine
layer. Stir fish mixture and divide between
cups or dishes. Place in a steaming basket and
position over a saucepan of boiling water.
Cover pan and steam for about 15 minutes
until just set in centre. Place on a warmed
serving plate, trickle coconut cream over top
and garnish with strips of red chilli.

Serves 2.

COCONUT FISH WITH GALANGAL

4 tablespoons vegetable oil
1 shallot, chopped
4 cm (1½ in) piece galangal, finely chopped
2 stalks lemon grass, finely chopped
1 small fresh red chilli, seeded and chopped
125 ml (4 fl oz/½ cup) coconut milk
2 teaspoons fish sauce
5 coriander sprigs
about 350 g (12 oz) white fish fillets, such as halibut,
   red snapper
1 small onion, sliced
freshly ground black pepper

In a wok, heat 1 tablespoon oil, add shallot,
galangal, lemon grass and chilli. Stir for 3
minutes until lightly coloured. Transfer to a
small blender, add coconut milk, fish sauce
and stalks from coriander sprigs and process
until well mixed. Place fish in a heatproof,
shallow round dish that fits over a saucepan,
and pour over spice sauce. Cover dish, place
over pan of boiling water and steam for 8-10
minutes until flesh flakes.

Meanwhile, heat remaining oil in a wok over
moderate heat, add onion and cook, stirring
occasionally, until browned. Using a slotted
spoon, transfer to absorbent kitchen paper.
Add coriander leaves to oil and fry for a few
seconds. Using a slotted spoon, transfer to
absorbent kitchen paper to drain. Scatter
fried onions and coriander over fish and grind
over plenty of black pepper.

Serves 3-4.

—FISH STIR-FRY WITH GINGER—

55 g (2 oz/½ cup) cornflour (cornstarch)
½ teaspoon ground ginger
1 teaspoon ground sea salt
750 g (1½ lb) haddock or other firm white fish fillets, skinned and cubed
3 tablespoons peanut oil
2.5 cm (1 in) piece fresh root ginger, peeled and finely chopped
4 spring onions (scallions), thinly sliced
1 tablespoon Chinese black vinegar or red wine vinegar
2 tablespoons rice wine or dry sherry
3 tablespoons dark soy sauce
1 teaspoon sugar
3 tablespoons fresh orange juice

In a bowl, mix together cornflour (cornstarch), ground ginger and salt, add fish in batches to coat evenly. In a wok, heat oil. Add fish and fry for 4 minutes, occasionally turning gently, until evenly browned.

In a bowl, mix together remaining ingredients, stir into wok, reduce the heat so the liquid just simmers, cover and cook for 4 minutes.

Serves 4.

—SWEET & SOUR SWORDFISH—

3 tablespoons light soy sauce
2 tablespoons dry sherry or rice wine
3 teaspoons wine or cider vinegar
1 tablespoon sugar
2 teaspoons medium chilli sauce or tomato ketchup (sauce)
450 g (1 lb) swordfish steaks, 2.5 cm (1 in) thick
3 tablespoons vegetable oil
1 red pepper (capsicum), cut into 2.5 cm (1 in) pieces
1 green pepper (capsicum), cut into 2.5 cm (1 in) pieces
4 spring onions, cut into 5 cm (2 in) pieces
3 teaspoons cornflour, dissolved in 1 tablespoon cold water
150 ml (5 fl oz/⅔ cup) fish or chicken stock

In a bowl, combine soy sauce, sherry or rice wine, vinegar, sugar and chilli sauce or tomato ketchup (sauce). Cut swordfish into strips and stir into marinade to coat. Leave to stand for 20 minutes. Heat the wok until very hot but not smoking, add 2 tablespoons vegetable oil and swirl to coat wok. With a slotted spoon, remove fish pieces from the marinade, draining off and reserving as much liquid as possible. Add fish to the wok and stir-fry for 2-3 minutes, until fish is firm. With a slotted spoon, remove fish strips to a bowl.

Add remaining oil to the wok. Add peppers (capsicums) and stir-fry for 2-3 minutes, until peppers begin to soften. Add spring onions and stir-fry for 1 more minute. Stir the cornflour mixture and add the reserved marinade, then stir in the stock until well blended. Pour into the wok and bring to the boil, stirring frequently. Simmer for 1-2 minutes until thickened. Return swordfish to the sauce and stir gently for 1 minute to heat through. Serve with rice and wild rice garnished with chives.

Serves 4.

—INDONESIAN-STYLE HALIBUT—

4 halibut fillets, about 175 g (6 oz) each
juice of 1 lime
2 teaspoons ground turmeric
115 ml (4 fl oz/½ cup) vegetable oil
1 clove garlic, finely chopped
1 cm (½ in) piece fresh root ginger, peeled and
    finely chopped
1 fresh chilli, seeded and chopped
1 onion, sliced lengthwise to form 'petals'
2 teaspoons ground coriander
150 ml (5 fl oz/⅔ cup) unsweetened coconut milk
1 teaspoon sugar
½ teaspoon salt
175 g (6 oz) mange tout (snow peas)
fresh coriander sprigs, to garnish

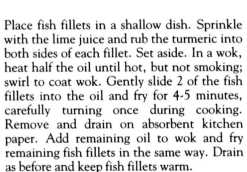

Place fish fillets in a shallow dish. Sprinkle with the lime juice and rub the turmeric into both sides of each fillet. Set aside. In a wok, heat half the oil until hot, but not smoking; swirl to coat wok. Gently slide 2 of the fish fillets into the oil and fry for 4-5 minutes, carefully turning once during cooking. Remove and drain on absorbent kitchen paper. Add remaining oil to wok and fry remaining fish fillets in the same way. Drain as before and keep fish fillets warm.

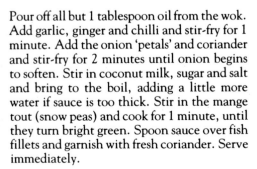

Pour off all but 1 tablespoon oil from the wok. Add garlic, ginger and chilli and stir-fry for 1 minute. Add the onion 'petals' and coriander and stir-fry for 2 minutes until onion begins to soften. Stir in coconut milk, sugar and salt and bring to the boil, adding a little more water if sauce is too thick. Stir in the mange tout (snow peas) and cook for 1 minute, until they turn bright green. Spoon sauce over fish fillets and garnish with fresh coriander. Serve immediately.

Serves 4.

——FISH WITH CHILLI SAUCE——

1 flat fish, such as pomfret, plump plaice or lemon sole,
    gutted and cleaned
vegetable oil for brushing
2 teaspoons vegetable oil
3 small dried red chillies, halved lengthwise
2 cloves garlic, finely chopped
1 teaspoon fish sauce
75 ml (2½ fl oz/⅓ cup) tamarind water, see page 12
1 teaspoon crushed palm sugar

Preheat grill. Brush fish lightly with oil, then grill for about 4 minutes a side until lightly coloured and flesh flakes when tested with the point of a knife. Using a fish slice, transfer to a warmed plate and keep warm.

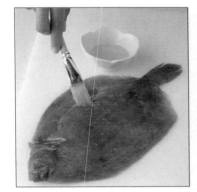

In a small saucepan, heat vegetable oil, add chillies and garlic and cook for 1 minute. Stir in remaining ingredients and simmer for 2-3 minutes until lightly thickened. Spoon over fish.

Serves 2.

STEAMED SEA BASS

1 kg (2¼ lb) sea bass, gutted, with head and
  tail left on
1 tablespoon Japanese rice wine or dry sherry
1 teaspoon sea salt
1 tablespoon peanut oil
2 tablespoons fermented black beans, rinsed, drained
  and coarsely chopped
1 clove garlic, finely chopped
1 cm (½ in) piece fresh root ginger, peeled and
  finely chopped
3 spring onions, thinly sliced
2 tablespoons soy sauce
115 ml (4 fl oz/½ cup) fish or chicken stock
6 teaspoons mild Chinese chilli sauce
1 teaspoon sesame oil
fresh coriander or spring onions, to garnish

With a sharp knife, make 3 or 4 diagonal
slashes 1 cm (½ in) deep on both sides of fish.
Sprinkle inside and out with wine or sherry
and salt. Place in an oval baking dish which
will fit in a wok. Allow to stand 20 minutes.
Place a wire rack or an inverted ramekin and
a plate in wok. Fill wok with 2.5 cm (1 in)
water and bring to the boil. Place dish with
the fish on the rack or ramekins and cover
tightly. Cook for 8-12 minutes, until fish
flakes easily. Remove fish from wok and keep
warm. Remove rack or ramekin and plate and
pour off water. Wipe wok dry and reheat.

Add peanut oil and swirl to coat wok. Add
the black beans, garlic and ginger and stir-fry
for 1 minute. Stir in the spring onions, soy
sauce and stock and bring to the boil; cook for
1 minute. Stir in the chilli sauce and sesame
oil and remove from the heat. Pour sauce
over fish and serve immediately, garnished
with fresh coriander or spring onions.

Serves 4.

TUNA WITH SPICY RELISH

2 tablespoons sesame oil
1 tablespoon light soy sauce
1 clove garlic, finely chopped
700 g (1½ lb) tuna steaks, 2.5 cm (1 in) thick,
  cut into chunks
2 tablespoons vegetable oil
225 g (8 oz) daikon (mooli), peeled and diced
225 g (8 oz) cucumber, peeled, seeded and diced
1 red pepper (capsicum), diced
1 red onion, coarsely chopped
1 fresh chilli, seeded and finely chopped
2 tablespoons lime juice
1 teaspoon sugar
1 tablespoon sesame seeds, toasted
lime wedges and fresh coriander sprigs, to garnish

In a shallow dish, combine 1 tablespoon
sesame oil with soy sauce and garlic. Add
tuna chunks and toss gently to coat. Allow to
stand for 15 minutes. Heat the wok until very
hot; add 1 tablespoon of the vegetable oil and
swirl to coat. Add daikon, cucumber, red
pepper (capsicum), red onion and fresh chilli
and stir-fry for 2-3 minutes until vegetables
begin to soften and turn a bright colour. Stir
in lime juice, sugar and remaining sesame oil
and cook for 30 seconds until sugar dissolves.
Remove to a bowl.

Add remaining vegetable oil to wok and,
working in batches, if necessary, add the fish
chunks and stir-fry gently for 2-3 minutes,
until firm. Arrange fish on 4 dinner plates
and sprinkle with the sesame seeds. Spoon
some of the warm relish onto each plate and
garnish with lime wedges and fresh coriander
sprigs. Serve with noodles.

Serves 4.

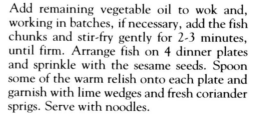

'MOCK' LOBSTER STIR-FRY

15 cm (6 in) stalk fresh lemon grass, trimmed
1 teaspoon tomato purée (paste)
1 tablespoon vegetable oil
1 tablespoon sesame oil
450 g (1 lb) monkfish tails, skinned and cut into
    chunks, or 450 g (1 lb) cooked lobster
3 cloves garlic, finely chopped
2.5 cm (1 in) fresh root ginger, peeled and chopped
1 onion, cut lengthwise into 'petals'
1 fresh chilli, seeded and finely chopped
2 tomatoes, peeled, seeded and chopped
1 teaspoon sugar
2 large spring onions, sliced into 2.5 cm (1 in) pieces
2 tablespoons fresh chopped coriander
1 tablespoon lime juice
lime wedges and coriander, to garnish

Crush lemon grass and cut into 2.5 cm (1 in) pieces. Place in a saucepan with 175 ml (6 fl oz/¾ cup) water and bring to the boil. Simmer for 3 minutes. Add tomato purée (paste); stir until dissolved. Set aside. Heat the oils in the wok until very hot. Add fish and stir-fry for 3-4 minutes, until firm. Transfer fish to a bowl. If using lobster, stir-fry for 1-2 minutes, then transfer to a bowl. Add garlic and ginger to wok and stir-fry for 10 seconds. Add onion and chilli and stir-fry for 1-2 minutes, until onion begins to soften. Add tomatoes, sugar and lemon grass mixture.

Add spring onions, chopped coriander and lime juice; cook for 1 minute until spring onions turn bright green. Return fish or lobster to wok and cook for 1 minute until it is heated through. Serve immediately, garnished with lime wedges and coriander. Accompany with noodles.

Serves 2.

Note: Monkfish (anglerfish) is often called 'poor man's lobster' due to its sweet flavour and firm, lobster-like texture.

FIVE-SPICE SALMON

1 teaspoon sesame oil
3 tablespoons soy sauce
3 tablespoons dry sherry or rice wine
1 tablespoon honey
1 tablespoon lime or lemon juice
1 teaspoon five-spice powder
700 g (1½ lb) salmon fillet, skinned and cut into
    2.5 cm (1 in) strips
2 egg whites
3 teaspoons cornflour
300 ml (10 fl oz/1¼ cups) vegetable oil
6 spring onions, sliced into 5 cm (2 in) pieces
115 ml (4 fl oz/½ cup) light fish or chicken
    stock or water
dash hot pepper sauce (optional)
lime wedges, to garnish

In a shallow baking dish, combine the sesame oil, soy sauce, sherry or wine, honey, lime or lemon juice and five-spice powder. Add salmon strips and toss gently to coat. Leave to stand for 30 minutes. With a slotted spoon, remove the salmon strips from marinade and pat dry with absorbent kitchen paper. Reserve marinade. In a small dish, beat egg whites and cornflour to make a batter. Add salmon strips and toss gently to coat completely.

Heat the vegetable oil in the wok until hot. Add the salmon in batches. Fry for 2-3 minutes until golden, turning once. Remove and drain on absorbent kitchen paper. Pour oil from wok and wipe wok clean. Pour marinade into wok and add spring onions, stock or water and pepper sauce, if using. Bring to the boil and simmer for 1-2 minutes. Add fish and turn gently to coat. Cook for 1 minute until hot. Garnish with lime and serve with noodles.

Serves 4.

POULTRY

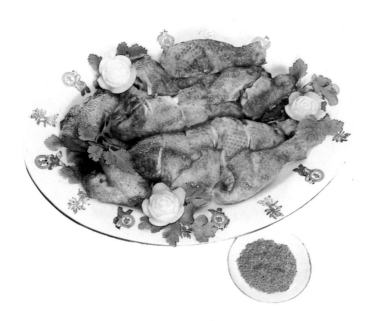

—CHICKEN IN COCONUT MILK—

—CHICKEN WITH CORIANDER—

8 black peppercorns, cracked
6 coriander roots, finely chopped
4.5 cm (1¾ in) piece galangal, thinly sliced
2 fresh green chillies, seeded and thinly sliced
625 ml (20 fl oz/2½ cups) coconut milk
grated peel 1 kaffir lime
4 kaffir lime leaves, shredded
1.35 kg (3 lb) chicken, cut into 8 pieces
1 tablespoon fish sauce
3 tablespoons lime juice
3 tablespoons chopped coriander leaves

Using a pestle and mortar or small blender, pound or mix together peppercorns, coriander roots and galangal.

6 coriander sprigs
1 tablespoon black peppercorns, crushed
2 cloves garlic, chopped
juice 1 lime
2 teaspoons fish sauce
4 large or 6 medium chicken drumsticks or thighs
lime wedges, to serve
Spring Onion (Scallion) Brushes, see page 15, to garnish

Using a pestle and mortar or small blender, pound or mix together coriander, peppercorns, garlic, lime juice and fish sauce; set aside.

In a wok, briefly heat peppercorn mixture, stirring, then stir in chillies, coconut milk, lime peel and leaves. Heat to just simmering point and add chicken portions. Adjust heat so liquid is barely moving, then cook gently for about 40-45 minutes until chicken is very tender and liquid reduced.

Using the point of a sharp knife, cut slashes in chicken. Spread spice mixture over chicken. Cover and set aside in a cool place for 2-3 hours, turning occasionally.

Stir in fish sauce and lime juice. Scatter coriander leaves over chicken and serve.

Serves 6-8.

Preheat grill. Grill chicken, basting and turning occasionally, for about 10 minutes until cooked through and golden. Serve with wedges of lime and garnish with spring onion (scallion) brushes.

Serves 2-6.

LEMON GRASS CURRY CHICKEN

BARBECUED CHICKEN

350 g (12 oz) boneless chicken, chopped into
  small pieces
1 tablespoon Red Curry Paste, see page 18
3 tablespoons vegetable oil
2 cloves garlic, finely chopped
1 tablespoon fish sauce
2 stalks lemon grass, finely chopped
5 kaffir lime leaves, shredded
½ teaspoon crushed palm sugar

Place chicken in a bowl, add curry paste and
stir to coat chicken; set aside for 30 minutes.

4 fresh red chillies, seeded and sliced
2 cloves garlic, chopped
5 shallots, finely sliced
2 teaspoons crushed palm sugar
125 ml (4 fl oz/½ cup) coconut cream, see page 10
2 teaspoons fish sauce
1 tablespoon tamarind water, see page 12
4 boneless chicken breasts
Thai holy basil leaves or coriander leaves, to garnish

Using a pestle and mortar or small blender,
pound chillies, garlic and shallots to a paste.
Work in sugar, then stir in coconut cream,
fish sauce and tamarind water.

In a wok, heat oil, add garlic and fry until
golden. Stir in chicken, then fish sauce,
lemon grass, lime leaves, sugar and 125 ml
(4 fl oz/½ cup) water.

Using the point of a sharp knife, cut 4 slashes
in chicken breast. Place chicken in a shallow
dish and pour over spice mixture. Turn to
coat, cover dish and set aside for 1 hour.

Adjust heat so liquid is barely moving and
cook for 15-20 minutes until chicken is
cooked through. If chicken becomes too dry,
add a little more water, but the final dish
should be quite dry.

Serves 3-4.

Preheat grill. Place chicken on a piece of foil
and grill for about 4 minutes a side, basting
occasionally, until cooked through. Garnish
with basil or coriander leaves.

Serves 4.

SPICED CHICKEN

5 shallots, chopped
3 cloves garlic, chopped
5 coriander roots, chopped
2 stalks lemon grass, chopped
2 fresh red chillies, seeded and chopped
4 cm (1½ in) piece fresh root ginger, finely chopped
1 teaspoon shrimp paste
1½ tablespoons vegetable oil
2 chicken legs, divided into thighs and drumsticks
1½ tablespoons tamarind water, see page 12

Using a pestle and mortar or small blender, pound or mix until smooth shallots, garlic, coriander, lemon grass, chillies, ginger and shrimp paste.

In a wok, heat oil, stir in spicy paste and cook, stirring, for 3-4 minutes. Stir in chicken pieces to coat evenly.

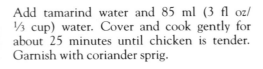

Add tamarind water and 85 ml (3 fl oz/ ⅓ cup) water. Cover and cook gently for about 25 minutes until chicken is tender. Garnish with coriander sprig.

Serves 3-4.

CHICKEN WITH BASIL LEAVES

2 tablespoons vegetable oil
2 cloves garlic, chopped
350 g (12 oz) skinned chicken breast, chopped
1 small onion, finely chopped
3 fresh red chillies, seeded and thinly sliced
20 Thai holy basil leaves
1 tablespoon fish sauce
4 tablespoons coconut milk
squeeze lime juice
Thai holy basil leaves and Chilli Flower, see page 15, to garnish

In a wok, heat 1 tablespoon oil, add garlic, chicken, onion and chillies and cook, stirring occasionally, for 3-5 minutes until cooked through.

Stir in basil leaves, fish sauce and coconut milk. Stir briefly over heat. Squeeze over lime juice. Serve garnished with basil leaves and chilli flower.

Serves 2-3.

—CHICKEN WITH GALANGAL—

450 g (1 lb) chicken breast meat
3 tablespoons vegetable oil
2 cloves garlic, finely chopped
1 onion, quartered and sliced
2.5 cm (1 in) piece galangal, finely chopped
8 pieces dried Chinese black mushrooms, soaked for 30 minutes, drained and chopped
1 fresh red chilli, seeded and cut into fine strips
1 tablespoon fish sauce
1½ teaspoons crushed palm sugar
1 tablespoon lime juice
12 Thai mint leaves
4 spring onions (scallions), including some green, chopped
Thai mint leaves, to garnish

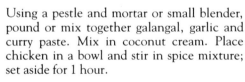
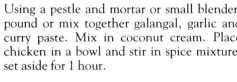

Using a sharp knife, cut chicken into 5.5 cm (2¼ in) long, 2.5 cm (1 in) wide pieces; set aside. In a wok, heat oil, add garlic and onion and cook, stirring occasionally, until golden. Stir in chicken and stir-fry for about 2 minutes.

Add galangal, mushrooms and chilli and stir-fry for 1 minute. Stir in fish sauce, sugar, lime juice, mint leaves, spring onions (scallions) and 3-4 tablespoons water. Cook, stirring, for about 1 minute. Transfer to a warmed serving dish and scatter over mint leaves.

Serves 4.

CHICKEN WITH PEANUT SAUCE

2.5 cm (1 in) piece galangal, chopped
2 cloves garlic, chopped
1½ tablespoons Fragrant Curry Paste, see page 19
4 tablespoons coconut cream, see page 10
450 g (1 lb) chicken breast meat, cut into large pieces
3 shallots, chopped
4 tablespoons dry-roasted peanuts, chopped
250 ml (8 fl oz/1 cup) coconut milk
½ teaspoon finely chopped dried red chilli
2 teaspoons fish sauce
freshly cooked broccoli, to serve

Using a pestle and mortar or small blender, pound or mix together galangal, garlic and curry paste. Mix in coconut cream. Place chicken in a bowl and stir in spice mixture; set aside for 1 hour.

Heat a wok, add shallots and coated chicken and stir-fry for 3-4 minutes. In a blender, mix peanuts with coconut milk, then stir into chicken with chilli and fish sauce. Cook gently for about 30 minutes until chicken is tender and thick sauce formed. Transfer to centre of a warmed serving plate and arrange cooked broccoli around.

Serves 4.

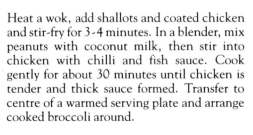

—CHICKEN WITH MANGE TOUT—

3 tablespoons vegetable oil
3 cloves garlic, chopped
1 dried red chilli, seeded and chopped
3 red shallots, chopped
2 tablespoons lime juice
2 teaspoons fish sauce
350 g (12 oz) chicken, finely chopped
1½ stalks lemon grass, chopped
1 kaffir lime leaf, sliced
175 g (6 oz) mange tout (snow peas)
1½ tablespoons coarsely ground browned rice,
   see page 12
3 spring onions (scallions), chopped
chopped coriander leaves, to garnish

In a wok, heat 2 tablespoons oil, add garlic and cook, stirring occasionally, until lightly browned. Stir in chilli, shallots, lime juice, fish sauce and 4 tablespoons water. Simmer for 1-2 minutes, then stir in chicken, lemon grass and lime leaf. Cook, stirring, for 2-3 minutes until chicken is just cooked through. Transfer to a warmed plate and keep warm.

Heat remaining oil in wok, add mange tout (snow peas) and stir-fry for 2-3 minutes until just tender. Transfer to a warmed serving plate. Return chicken to wok. Add rice and spring onions (scallions). Heat for about 1 minute, then transfer to serving plate. Garnish with chopped coriander.

Serves 3-4.

—— YELLOW BEAN CHICKEN ——

2 egg whites
4 teaspoons cornflour
700 g (1½ lb) skinned and boned chicken breasts or
   thighs, cut into 2.5 cm (1 in) cubes
115 ml (4 fl oz/½ cup) peanut oil
4 spring onions, sliced
2 stalks celery, thinly sliced
1 green pepper (capsicum), diced
1 teaspoon finely chopped fresh root ginger
1 teaspoon crushed chillies
1 teaspoon sugar
4 teaspoons yellow bean paste
4 teaspoons dry sherry or rice wine
150 g (5 oz/1 cup) cashew nuts, toasted
lemon wedges, to garnish

In a medium bowl, beat egg whites with the cornflour. Add chicken cubes, tossing to coat well. Refrigerate for 10-15 minutes. In the wok, heat peanut oil until very hot and swirl to coat wok. Using a slotted spoon, and working in 2 batches, lift out chicken cubes and add to wok. Stir-fry quickly to keep cubes from sticking. Cook chicken cubes for 2-3 minutes until just golden. Remove to absorbent kitchen paper to drain and pour off all but 2 tablespoons oil. (Reserve oil for future frying or discard.)

Add spring onions, celery, green pepper (capsicum) and ginger and stir-fry for 2-3 minutes until onion and pepper (capsicum) begin to soften. Stir in the crushed chillies, sugar, yellow bean paste, dry sherry or rice wine and the cashew nuts, tossing until sugar dissolves. Add chicken cubes and toss to coat; cook for 30 seconds. Serve immediately, garnished with lemon wedges and accompanied by a salad.

Serves 4.

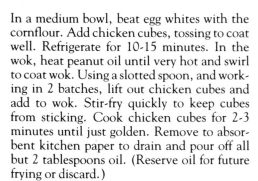

FIVE-SPICE CHICKEN

500 ml (16 fl oz/2 cups) peanut oil
1 tablespoon dark soy sauce
1 tablespoon brandy
½ teaspoon Chinese five-spice powder
½ teaspoon brown sugar
1 cm (½ in) piece fresh root ginger, peeled and finely
    chopped
2 spring onions (scallions), finely chopped
2 cloves garlic, finely chopped
500 g (1 lb) boned chicken breasts, cubed
1 large egg, beaten
55 g (2 oz/½ cup) cornflour (cornstarch)

In a large bowl, mix together 2 tablespoons peanut oil, soy sauce, brandy, five-spice powder, sugar, ginger, spring onions (scallions) and garlic. Stir in chicken cubes to coat evenly. Leave for at least 1 hour. Stir in beaten egg. Put cornflour (cornstarch) on a plate, roll each chicken cube in cornflour (cornstarch) until evenly coated.

In a wok, heat remaining oil over a moderate heat, add chicken and deep-fry for 4 minutes. Increase heat and fry for 2 minutes until golden and cooked through. Using a slotted spoon, lift chicken from oil and drain on absorbent kitchen paper.

Serves 4.

BANG BANG CHICKEN

55 ml (2 fl oz/¼ cup) peanut oil
3 carrots, cut into julienne strips
1 fresh chilli, seeded and chopped
225 g (8 oz) beansprouts, trimmed
½ cucumber, seeded and cut into julienne strips
800 g (1¾ lb) skinned and boned chicken breasts,
    cut into shreds
2.5 cm (1 in) fresh ginger, cut in julienne strips
2 cloves garlic, finely chopped
4 spring onions, thinly sliced
9 teaspoons cider vinegar or rice vinegar
2 tablespoons dry sherry or rice wine
1 tablespoon sugar
1 teaspoon Chinese chilli sauce
150 ml (5 fl oz/⅔ cup) chicken stock
3 tablespoons each light soy sauce and tahini

Heat wok until hot. Add 2 tablespoons peanut oil and swirl to coat wok. Add carrots and chilli and stir-fry for 2-3 minutes. Remove to a bowl. Stir-fry beansprouts for 1 minute and remove to bowl. Add cucumber to bowl. Heat remaining oil in wok and add chicken. Working in 2 batches, stir-fry for 2-3 minutes until the chicken is white and the juices run clear. Remove to another bowl. Increase heat, add ginger and garlic to wok and stir-fry for 1 minute. Add spring onions and stir-fry for 1 minute. Add remaining ingredients and stir-fry until sauce is smooth and thick.

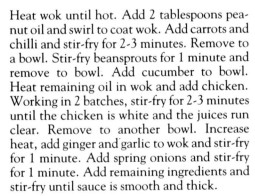

Pour half the sauce over carrot mixture and remaining sauce over chicken; toss each mixture well. Spoon chicken onto centre of a serving dish, then spoon vegetables around chicken. Serve with rice or noodles.

Serves 6.

Note: Garnish with sesame seeds or chopped peanuts and coriander, if wished.

LEMON CHICKEN

2 egg whites
7 teaspoons cornflour
575 g (1¼ lb) skinned and boned chicken breasts,
    cut into thin strips
115 ml (4 fl oz/½ cup) vegetable oil
1 onion, thinly sliced
1 clove garlic, finely chopped
1 red pepper (capsicum), thinly sliced
150 ml (5 fl oz/⅔ cup) chicken stock
grated rind and juice of 1 lemon
1 tablespoon sugar
1 tablespoon light soy sauce
1 tablespoon rice wine or dry sherry
dash hot pepper sauce
fresh chives, to garnish

In a medium bowl, beat egg whites with 4 teaspoons cornflour. Add the chicken strips and toss to coat well. Refrigerate for 10-15 minutes. In the wok, heat the vegetable oil until very hot and swirl to coat wok. Using tongs or a fork, add the chicken strips a few at a time. Stir-fry quickly to keep strips from sticking. Cook chicken strips for 2-3 minutes until just golden. Remove to absorbent kitchen paper to drain and pour off all but 1 tablespoon oil. (Reserve oil for future frying or discard.)

Add onion, garlic and red pepper (capsicum) to the wok. Stir-fry for 1-2 minutes until onion begins to soften. Add chicken stock, lemon rind and juice, sugar, soy sauce, wine or sherry and a few drops hot pepper sauce. Dissolve remaining cornflour in 2 table-spoons water and stir into the sauce. Cook for 30 seconds until sauce thickens. Add chicken strips and toss to coat. Cook for 1 minute, until chicken is heated through. Garnish with chives and serve with boiled rice.

Serves 4.

CHICKEN IN BLACK BEAN SAUCE

250 ml (8 fl oz/1 cup) peanut oil
500 g (1 lb) boned chicken breasts, cubed
10 button mushrooms, halved
½ red pepper (capsicum), seeded and diced
½ green pepper (capsicum), seeded and diced
4 spring onions (scallions), finely chopped
2 carrots, thinly sliced
2 tablespoons dried black beans, washed
1 cm (½ in) fresh root ginger, peeled and grated
1 clove garlic, finely chopped
2 tablespoons rice wine or dry sherry
250 ml (8 fl oz/1 cup) Chinese Chicken Stock,
    see page 22
1 tablespoon light soy sauce
2 teaspoons cornflour (cornstarch) dissolved in
    1 tablespoon water

In a wok, heat oil until smoking, add chicken cubes and deep-fry for 2 minutes. Using a slotted spoon, lift chicken from oil and drain on absorbent kitchen paper. Pour oil from wok, leaving just 2 tablespoonsful. Add mushrooms to wok and stir-fry for 1 minute. Add red and green peppers (capsicum), spring onions (scallions) and carrots, stir-fry for 3 minutes.

In a bowl, mash black beans with ginger, garlic and rice wine or dry sherry, stir into wok then stir in stock and soy sauce. Cook for another 2 minutes. Stir in cornflour (corn-starch) mixture and bring to the boil, stirring. Stir in chicken and heat through gently.

Serves 4.

TANGERINE CHICKEN WINGS

CRISPY-SKIN CHICKEN

1 onion, thinly sliced
2.5 cm (1 in) piece fresh root ginger, peeled and
    thinly sliced
1 teaspoon sea salt
4 tablespoons dry sherry or rice wine
4 tablespoons soy sauce
16 chicken wings, wing tips removed
1 large tangerine
70 ml (2½ fl oz/⅓ cup) vegetable oil
2 fresh chillies, seeded and chopped
4 spring onions, thinly sliced
2 teaspoons sugar
3 teaspoons wine vinegar
1 teaspoon sesame oil
fresh coriander sprigs, to garnish

1.5 kg (3 lb) chicken
salt
1 tablespoon golden syrup
4 tablespoons plus 1 teaspoon sea salt
3½ teaspoons Chinese five-spice powder
2 tablespoons rice vinegar
925 ml (30 fl oz/3¾ cups) vegetable oil

Bring a large saucepan of salted water to the
boil. Lower in chicken, return to the boil,
then remove pan from heat, cover tightly and
leave the chicken in the water for 30 minutes.

In a large shallow baking dish, combine
onion, ginger, salt, 1 tablespoon sherry or
rice wine and 1 tablespoon soy sauce. Add
chicken wings and toss to coat well. Leave
to stand 30 minutes. Remove rind from
tangerine and slice thinly. Squeeze 2-3 tablespoons tangerine juice and reserve. Heat oil
in wok until hot and swirl to coat wok.
Remove chicken from the marinade, return-
ing any onion or ginger sticking to it. Working in 2 batches, add chicken wings to wok.
Fry for 3-4 minutes until golden, turning
once. Drain on absorbent kitchen paper.

Drain chicken, dry with absorbent kitchen
paper and leave in a cold dry place for at least
12 hours. In a small bowl, mix together
golden syrup, 1 teaspoon salt, ½ teaspoon
five-spice powder and rice vinegar. Brush
over chicken and leave in the refrigerator for
20 minutes. Repeat until all the coating is
used. Refrigerate the chicken for at least 4
hours to allow the coating to dry thoroughly
on the skin.

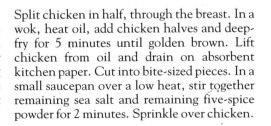

Pour off all but 1 tablespoon oil from wok.
Add chillies, spring onions and tangerine
rind and stir-fry for 30-40 seconds. Pour in
reserved marinade with the onion and ginger
slices. Add sugar, vinegar and remaining
sherry or rice wine, soy sauce and tangerine
juice. Add the chicken wings and toss to coat
well; cook for 1 minute until heated through.
Drizzle with sesame oil and garnish with
coriander sprigs. Serve with noodles tossed in
sesame oil and sesame seeds, if wished.

Serves 4.

Split chicken in half, through the breast. In a
wok, heat oil, add chicken halves and deep-
fry for 5 minutes until golden brown. Lift
chicken from oil and drain on absorbent
kitchen paper. Cut into bite-sized pieces. In a
small saucepan over a low heat, stir together
remaining sea salt and remaining five-spice
powder for 2 minutes. Sprinkle over chicken.

Serves 4.

— SZECHUAN CHICKEN LIVERS —

— JAPANESE CHICKEN LIVERS —

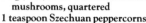

25 g (1 oz) dried Chinese mushrooms or 115 g (4 oz)
   mushrooms, quartered
1 teaspoon Szechuan peppercorns
2 tablespoons vegetable oil
450 g (1 lb) chicken livers, trimmed and cut in half
2.5 cm (1 in) piece fresh root ginger, peeled and
   finely chopped
2 cloves garlic, finely chopped
4-6 spring onions, thinly sliced
2 teaspoons cornflour, dissolved in 2 tablespoons water
2 tablespoons soy sauce
2 tablespoons rice wine or dry sherry
½ teaspoon sugar
spring onions, to garnish

2 tablespoons light soy sauce
2 tablespoons mirin or dry sherry mixed with
   ½ teaspoon sugar
450 g (1 lb) chicken livers, trimmed and cut in half
2 tablespoons vegetable oil
1 green pepper (capsicum), diced
4 spring onions, sliced
1 clove garlic, finely chopped
2.5 cm (1 in) piece fresh root ginger, peeled and
   finely chopped
¼ teaspoon cayenne pepper
2 tablespoons sugar
3 tablespoons dark soy sauce
1 teaspoon sesame oil
julienne strips of radish, to garnish (optional)

If using dried mushrooms, place in a bowl, cover with warm water and soak for 20-25 minutes. Using a slotted spoon, carefully remove mushrooms from water, to avoid disturbing any grit which has sunk to the bottom. Reserve liquid. Squeeze mushrooms dry, then cut off and discard stems. Heat wok until hot. Add Szechuan peppercorns and dry-fry for 2-3 minutes until very fragrant. Pour into bowl to cool. When cold, crush in a mortar and pestle or grind in a spice grinder. Set aside.

In a shallow dish, combine the light soy sauce, mirin or sweetened sherry and chicken livers. Leave to marinate for 20-30 minutes, stirring occasionally. Heat the wok until hot. Add oil and swirl to coat wok. With a slotted spoon, remove chicken livers from the marinade and add to wok. Stir-fry for 3-4 minutes, until beginning to brown. Add green pepper (capsicum), spring onions, garlic and ginger and stir-fry for a further 1-2 minutes. The chicken livers should be browned, but still pink inside.

Heat wok until hot. Add oil and swirl to coat. Pat livers dry and stir-fry for 2-3 minutes. Add ginger, garlic, mushrooms and spring onions. Stir-fry for 2 minutes, until livers are brown. Add 2 tablespoons mushroom liquid if using dried mushrooms or 2 tablespoons water if using fresh mushrooms, to dissolved cornflour. Stir into wok with soy sauce, wine or sherry, peppercorns and sugar. Stir until thickened. Garnish with spring onions and serve with rice.

Stir in cayenne pepper, sugar and dark soy sauce and toss to coat well. Drizzle with the sesame oil and serve immediately, garnished with radish, if wished.

Serves 4.

Serves 4.

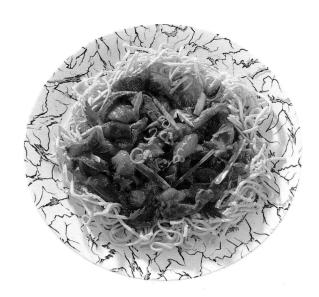

— DUCK WITH GREEN PEPPERS —

1 egg white
3 tablespoons cornflour (cornstarch)
sea salt
500 g (1 lb) boned duck breasts, cubed
625 ml (20 fl oz/2½ cups) peanut oil
2 green peppers (capsicums), seeded and cut into
  2.5 cm (1 in) squares
2 tablespoons light soy sauce
3 teaspoons rice wine or dry sherry
1 teaspoon brown sugar
115 ml (4 fl oz/½ cup) Chinese Chicken Stock, see
  page 22
1 teaspoon sesame oil
white pepper

In a bowl, whisk together egg white, corn-flour (cornstarch) and 1 teaspoon salt. Stir in duck cubes to mix thoroughly. Leave for 20 minutes. In a wok, heat peanut oil until very hot. Add duck and deep-fry for about 4 minutes, until crisp.

Remove and drain on absorbent kitchen paper. Add peppers (capsicums) to wok and deep-fry for 2 minutes then drain on absorbent kitchen paper. Pour oil from wok, leaving 2 tablespoonsful. Add soy sauce, rice wine or dry sherry, sugar, stock, sesame oil, and salt and pepper to taste. Boil, then add cooked duck, peppers (capsicums) and gently heat through.

Serves 4.

— DUCK WITH PLUMS —

2 tablespoons vegetable oil
700 g (1½ lb) duckling breast fillets, skinned and
  excess fat removed, cut crosswise into thin strips
225 g (8 oz) red plums, stoned and thinly sliced
55 ml (2 fl oz/¼ cup) port
6 teaspoons wine vinegar
grated rind and juice of 1 orange
2 tablespoons Chinese plum or duck sauce
4 spring onions, cut into thin strips
1 tablespoon soy sauce
3-4 whole cloves
small piece cinnamon stick
½ teaspoon Chinese chilli sauce (or to taste)
fresh parsley and grated orange rind, to garnish

Heat the wok until hot. Add oil and swirl to coat wok. Add duckling breast strips and stir-fry for 3-4 minutes until golden. Remove to a bowl. Add plums, port, wine vinegar, rind and juice of the orange, plum or duck sauce, spring onions, soy sauce, cloves, cinnamon stick and chilli sauce to taste. Bring to simmering point and cook gently for 4-5 minutes until plums begin to soften.

Return duckling strips to wok and stir-fry for 2 minutes until duck is heated through and sauce is thickened. Garnish with parsley and grated orange rind. Serve with noodles or rice tossed with sesame seeds.

Serves 4.

PEKING DUCK

1.75 kg (4 lb) oven-ready duck
1 tablespoon honey
3 tablespoons dark soy sauce
1 tablespoon sesame oil
edible red food colouring, if desired
2 tablespoons water
PANCAKES:
500 g (1 lb/4 cups) plain (all-purpose) flour
250 ml (8 fl oz/1 cup) boiling water
90 ml (3 fl oz/⅓ cup) cold water
1 teaspoon sesame oil
TO SERVE:
hoisin sauce
6 spring onions (scallions), cut into long shreds
½ cucumber, cut into long shreds

Divide dough in half on a lightly floured surface, roll each half to a long roll 5 cm (2 in) in diameter. Cut into 2.5 cm (1 in) lengths.

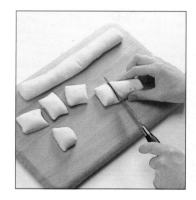

Place the duck in a colander in the sink. Pour over boiling water; repeat twice. Hang duck overnight in a cold airy place, or place on a rack in the refrigerator. Next morning, in a small bowl, mix together honey, soy sauce, sesame oil and colouring, if used. Place duck on a rack in a roasting tin, making sure the neck opening is closed. Brush evnly with honey mixture and leave for at least 1 hour. Pre-heat oven to 200C (400F/Gas 6).

Flatten each piece with the palm of the hand. Lightly brush tops with sesame oil and place two pieces together, oiled sides facing. Roll out each pair to 15 cm (6 in) pancakes.

Stir water into remaining honey mixture and pour through the vent, into the duck. With a meat skewer or wooden cocktail sticks, secure vent. Roast duck, 1½ hours, until juices run clear. Remove duck from oven and leave in a warm place for 10 minutes before carving.

Meanwhile, make the pancakes. Sift flour into a bowl and gradually stir in boiling water; mix well. Stir in cold water to form a ball. On a floured surface, knead until smooth. Return to bowl, cover with a damp cloth and leave for 15 minutes.

Place a dry, non-stick frying pan over a moderate heat and fry each pancake for 20-30 seconds until beginning to bubble. Turn over pancake and cook for a further 10-15 seconds until light browned. Remove from pan and carefully separate the top and bottom. Keep warm, interleaved with greaseproof paper.

Serve the carved duck on a warm plate with the stack of pancakes, and with hoisin sauce, spring onions (scallions) and cucumber in separate bowls.

Serves 4.

MEAT

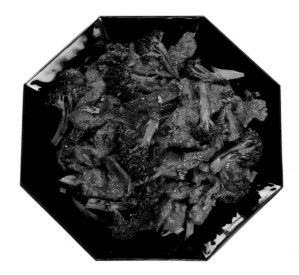

LAMB WITH SPINACH

3 tablespoons soy sauce
¼ teaspoon five-spice powder
2.5 cm (1 in) piece fresh root ginger, peeled and cut
   into julienne strips
2 cloves garlic, finely chopped
700 g (1½ lb) lamb fillet, cut crosswise into thin strips
1 tablespoon sesame oil
1 fresh red chilli, seeded and thinly sliced
8 spring onions, cut into 5 cm (2 in) pieces
1 mango, peeled and cut into 1 cm (½ in) thick pieces
175 g (6 oz) fresh baby spinach leaves,
   washed and dried
3 tablespoons dry sherry or rice wine
1 teaspoon cornflour dissolved in 1 tablespoon water

In a shallow baking dish, combine soy sauce, five-spice powder, ginger and garlic. Add lamb strips and toss to coat well. Leave to marinate for 1 hour, covered, stirring occasionally. Heat the wok until very hot. Add sesame oil and swirl to coat. With a slotted spoon and working in 2 batches, add lamb to wok, draining off and reserving as much marinade as possible. Stir-fry lamb for 2-3 minutes until browned on all sides. Remove to a bowl. Add chilli to oil remaining in wok and stir-fry for 1 minute.

Add spring onions and mango and stir-fry for 1 minute. Stir in spinach leaves, reserved lamb, dry sherry or rice wine and reserved marinade. Stir cornflour mixture and stir into wok. Stir-fry for 1 minute, tossing all ingredients until spinach wilts and lamb is lightly glazed with sauce. Serve with potatoes or noodles.

Serves 4.

LAMB WITH CORIANDER

500 g (1 lb) lamb fillet, cut into thin strips
1 tablespoon cornflour (cornstarch)
1 teaspoon granulated sugar
1 teaspoon sesame oil
2 tablespoons peanut oil
175 g (6 oz) broccoli florets, sliced
3 dried black winter mushrooms, soaked in hot water
   for 25 minutes, drained
2 spring onions (scallions), chopped
1 clove garlic, finely chopped
2 teaspoons rice wine or dry sherry
1 tablespoon dark soy sauce
1 tablespoon finely chopped fresh coriander

Place lamb in a dish. In a bowl, mix together cornflour (cornstarch), sugar and sesame oil and spoon over the lamb; stir to well-coat lamb. Leave for 30 minutes.

   In a wok, heat peanut oil, add lamb and stir-fry for 2 minutes. Remove lamb from wok and keep warm.

Add broccoli, mushrooms, spring onions (scallions) and garlic and stir-fry for about 5 minutes until broccoli is just tender. Stir in rice wine or dry sherry, soy sauce, lamb and coriander. Stir over a very high heat for 1 minute.

Serves 4.

—CHINESE BARBECUED LAMB—   —HUNAN LAMB STIR-FRY—

2 small eggs, beaten
85 g (3 oz/¾ cup) plain (all purpose) flour
1 teaspoon sea salt
½ teaspoon ground black pepper
1 teaspoon ground Szechuan pepper
4 spring onions (scallions), finely chopped
2 medium tomatoes, seeded and finely chopped
500 g (1 lb) lamb fillet, cut into cubes
4 teaspoons sesame seeds

In a bowl, mix together all ingredients, except lamb and sesame seeds. Stir in lamb to coat, cover and leave in a cool place for 4 hours.

Preheat grill or barbecue. Spread sesame seeds out on a plate. Roll lamb cubes in sesame seeds to coat evenly.

Thread cubes on to skewers and sprinkle on any remaining sesame seeds. Grill or barbecue for 4-5 minutes, turning frequently, until tender.

Serves 4.

---

1 egg white, lightly beaten
2 tablespoons cornflour (cornstarch)
ground white pepper to taste
500 g (1 lb) lamb fillet, thinly sliced
625 ml (20 fl oz/2½ cups) vegetable oil
3 slices fresh root ginger, peeled and finely chopped
85 g (3 oz) canned bamboo shoots, drained and chopped
1 small red pepper (capsicum), seeded and cut into thin strips
3 spring onions (scallions), finely chopped
55 g (2 oz) cucumber, cut into strips
2 teaspoons rice wine or dry sherry

In a small bowl, mix together egg white, cornflour (cornstarch), salt and pepper. Stir lamb slices in mixture to evenly coat. Leave for 30 minutes. In a wok, heat oil, add lamb in batches, keeping slices separate, and deep-fry lamb for 2 minutes. Using a slotted spoon, lift lamb from oil and drain on absorbent kitchen paper.

Pour oil from wok, leaving just 2 tablespoonsful. Add ginger, bamboo shoots, pepper (capsicum), spring onions (scallions) and cucumber and stir-fry for 4 minutes. Add lamb and toss over a high heat for 1 minute. Stir in rice wine or dry sherry.

Serves 4.

PORK WITH WATER CHESTNUTS

1½ tablespoons vegetable oil
4 cloves garlic, chopped
2 fresh red chillies, seeded and finely chopped
350 g (12 oz) lean pork, cubed
10 canned water chestnuts, chopped
1 teaspoon fish sauce
freshly ground black pepper
3 tablespoons chopped coriander leaves
6 spring onions (scallions), chopped
3-4 Spring Onion (Scallion) Brushes, see page 15, to garnish

In a wok, heat oil, add garlic and chillies and cook, stirring occasionally, until garlic becomes golden.

Stir in pork and stir-fry for about 2 minutes until almost cooked through. Add water chestnuts, heat for 2 minutes, then stir in fish sauce, 4 tablespoons water and add plenty of black pepper. Stir in coriander and spring onions (scallions). Serve garnished with spring onion (scallion) brushes.

Serves 3-4.

BARBECUED SPARE RIBS

2 tablespoons chopped coriander stalks
3 cloves garlic, chopped
1 teaspoon black peppercorns, cracked
1 teaspoon grated kaffir lime peel
1 tablespoon Green Curry Paste, see page 18
2 teaspoons fish sauce
1½ teaspoons crushed palm sugar
185 ml (6 fl oz/¾ cup) coconut milk
900 g (2 lb) pork spare ribs, trimmed
Spring Onion (Scallion) Brushes, see page 15, to garnish

Using a pestle and mortar or small blender, pound or mix together coriander, garlic, peppercorns, lime peel, curry paste, fish sauce and sugar. Stir in coconut milk. Place spare ribs in a shallow dish and pour over spiced coconut mixture. Cover and leave in a cool place for 3 hours, basting occasionally.

Preheat a barbecue or moderate grill. Cook ribs for about 5 minutes a side, until cooked through and brown, basting occasionally with coconut mixture. Garnish with spring onion (scallion) brushes.

Serves 4-6.

Note: The ribs can also be cooked on a rack in a roasting tin in an oven preheated to 200C (400F/Gas 6) for 45-60 minutes, basting occasionally.

PORK SATAY

350 g (12 oz) lean pork, cubed
juice 1 lime
1 stalk lemon grass, finely chopped
1 clove garlic, chopped
2 tablespoons vegetable oil
SAUCE:
4 tablespoons vegetable oil
85 g (3 oz/½ cup) raw shelled peanuts
2 stalks lemon grass, chopped
2 fresh red chillies, seeded and sliced
3 shallots, chopped
2 cloves garlic, chopped
1 teaspoon fish paste
2 teaspoons crushed palm sugar
315 ml (10 fl oz/1¼ cups) coconut milk
juice ½ lime

Meanwhile, make sauce. Over a high heat, heat 1 tablespoon oil in a wok, add nuts and cook, stirring constantly, for 2 minutes. Using a slotted spoon, transfer to absorbent kitchen paper to drain. Using a pestle and mortar or small blender, grind to a paste. Remove and set aside.

Divide pork between 4 skewers and lay them in a shallow dish. In a bowl, mix together lime juice, lemon grass, garlic and oil. Pour over pork, turn to coat, cover and set aside in a cool place for 1 hour, turning occasionally.

Using a pestle and mortar or small blender, pound or mix lemon grass, chillies, shallots, garlic and fish paste to a smooth paste.

Preheat grill. Remove pork from dish, allowing excess liquid to drain off. Grill, turning frequently and basting, for 8-10 minutes.

Heat remaining oil in wok, add spice mixture and cook, stirring, for 2 minutes. Stir in peanut paste, sugar and coconut milk. Bring to boil, stirring, then adjust heat so sauce simmers. Add lime juice and simmer, stirring, for 5-10 minutes until thickened. Serve in a warmed bowl to accompany pork. Garnish with carrot flowers, see page 16, and lettuce leaves.

Serves 4.

—PORK & BAMBOO SHOOTS—

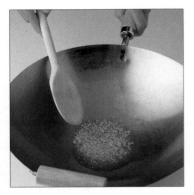

2 tablespoons vegetable oil
4 cloves garlic, very finely chopped
350 g (12 oz) lean pork, very finely chopped
115 g (4 oz) canned bamboo shoots, chopped or sliced
4 tablespoons peanuts, coarsely chopped
2 teaspoons fish sauce
freshly ground black pepper
4 large spring onions (scallions), thinly sliced
Thai holy basil sprig, to garnish

In a wok, heat oil, add garlic and fry, stirring occasionally, for about 3 minutes until lightly coloured.

Add pork and stir-fry for 2 minutes. Add bamboo shoots and continue to stir for a further minute.

Stir in peanuts, fish sauce, plenty of black pepper and half of spring onions (scallions). Transfer to a warmed serving plate and sprinkle over remaining spring onions (scallions) and basil sprig.

Serves 4.

—MIXED VEGETABLES & PORK—

225 g (8 oz) lean pork, finely chopped
freshly ground black pepper
2 tablespoons vegetable oil
3 cloves garlic, finely chopped
450 g (1 lb) prepared mixed vegetables, such as mange
  tout (snow peas), broccoli flowerets, red pepper
  (capsicum) and courgettes (zucchini)
1 tablespoon fish sauce
½ teaspoon crushed palm sugar
3 spring onions (scallions), finely chopped

In a bowl, mix together pork and plenty of black pepper. Set aside for 30 minutes.

In a wok or frying pan, heat oil, add garlic and cook, stirring occasionally, for 2-3 minutes, then stir in pork.

Stir briefly until pork changes colour. Stir in mixed vegetables, then fish sauce, sugar and 125 ml (4 fl oz/½ cup) water. Stir for 3-4 minutes until mange tout (snow peas) are bright green and vegetables still crisp. Stir in spring onions (scallions).

Serves 4.

—PORK WITH SPRING ONIONS—

—COCONUT PORK WITH LIME—

625 ml (20 fl oz/2½ cups) coconut milk
450 g (1 lb) lean pork, cut into 2.5 cm (1 in) cubes
1 tablespoon fish sauce
½ teaspoon crushed palm sugar
100 g (3½ oz/1 cup) skinned peanuts
3 fresh red chillies, seeded and chopped
3 cm (1¼ in) piece galangal, chopped
4 cloves garlic
1 stalk lemon grass, chopped
4 tablespoons coconut cream, see page 10
8 spring onions (scallions), chopped
1 kg (2 lb) young spinach leaves
warmed coconut cream and dry-roasted peanuts,
    to serve

6 pork escalopes, about 115 g (4 oz) each
1 cm (½ in) piece fresh root ginger, peeled and grated
2 teaspoons ground cumin
1 teaspoon ground coriander
1 teaspoon chilli powder (to taste)
1 teaspoon paprika
½ teaspoon salt
2-3 tablespoons vegetable oil
1 onion, cut lengthwise in half and thinly sliced
3-4 cloves garlic, finely chopped
300 ml (10 fl oz/1¼ cups) unsweetened coconut milk
grated rind and juice of 1 large lime
1 small Chinese cabbage, shredded
lime slices and coriander leaves, to garnish

In a wok, heat coconut milk just to simmering point, adjust heat so liquid barely moves. Add pork and cook for about 25 minutes until very tender. Meanwhile, using a small blender or food processor, mix fish sauce, sugar, peanuts, chillies, galangal, garlic and lemon grass to a paste. In another wok, or a frying pan, heat coconut cream until oil separates. Add spring onions (scallions) and peanut paste and cook, stirring frequently, for 2-3 minutes.

Place escalopes between 2 sheets of greaseproof paper. Pound to a 0.5 cm (¼ in) thickness. Cut into strips. In a large, shallow dish, combine ginger, cumin, coriander, chilli powder, paprika and salt. Stir in pork strips and leave to stand for 15 minutes. Heat wok until very hot. Add half the oil and swirl to coat wok. Add half the pork and stir-fry for 2-3 minutes. Remove to a plate and keep warm. Cook remaining strips using remaining oil. Keep warm. Pour off all but 1 tablespoon oil from the wok.

Stir in milk from pork and boil until lightly thickened. Pour over pork, stir and cook for 5 minutes more. Rinse spinach leaves, then pack into a saucepan with just water left on them. Gently cook for about 3 minutes until just beginning to wilt. Arrange on a warmed serving plate. Spoon pork and sauce onto centre. Trickle over coconut cream and scatter over dry-roasted peanuts.

Serves 4-6.

Add onion and garlic to wok; stir-fry for 2-3 minutes until onion is softened. Slowly add coconut milk. Bring to simmering point but do not boil. Stir in lime rind and juice and shredded cabbage. Simmer gently for 5-7 minutes, stirring frequently, until cabbage is tender and sauce slightly thickened. Add pork and cook, covered, for 1-2 minutes until heated through. Arrange pork and cabbage on plates and garnish with lime slices and coriander. Serve with noodles.

Serves 6.

–PORK WITH MELON & MANGO–

——INDONESIAN-STYLE PORK——

1 small Galia or ½ Honeydew melon, cut into
   julienne strips
1 slightly under-ripe mango, peeled and cut into
   julienne strips
salt and freshly ground black pepper
1 tablespoon sugar
juice of 1 lime or lemon
2 tablespoons sesame oil
225 g (8 oz) pork fillet, cut into shreds
4-6 spring onions, thinly sliced
2 cloves garlic, finely chopped
5 tablespoons nam pla (fish sauce)
1 tablespoon cider vinegar
½ teaspoon crushed chillies
chopped peanuts and chopped coriander, to garnish

In a medium bowl, toss melon and mango
strips with the salt and pepper to taste, sugar
and lime or lemon juice. Set aside. Heat the
wok until very hot. Add oil and swirl to coat,
add shredded pork and stir-fry for 2-3 minutes
until golden. With a slotted spoon, remove
to absorbent kitchen paper and drain.

To the oil remaining in the wok, add spring
onions and garlic and stir-fry for 1 minute.
Stir in the nam pla (fish sauce), vinegar and
chillies and salt and pepper if necessary. Add
the reserved pork and melon and mango,
together with any juices. Toss to mix ingredients and heat through. Spoon onto a
shallow serving dish and sprinkle with
chopped peanuts and coriander. Serve hot
or warm with noodles or shredded Chinese
cabbage.

Serves 2.

1 tablespoon seasoned flour
575 g (1¼ lb) pork fillet, cut into small cubes
2-3 tablespoons vegetable oil
1 onion, cut lengthwise in half and thinly sliced
2 cloves garlic, finely chopped
2.5 cm (1 in) piece fresh root ginger, peeled and
   cut into julienne strips
½ teaspoon sambal oelek (see Note) or
   Chinese chilli sauce
55 ml (2 fl oz/¼ cup) Indonesian soy sauce or dark soy
   sauce sweetened with 1 tablespoon sugar
coriander leaves, to garnish

In a medium bowl, combine seasoned flour
and pork cubes and toss to coat well. Shake to
remove any excess flour.

Heat the wok until very hot. Add 2 tablespoons of the oil and swirl to coat wok. Add
pork cubes and stir-fry for 3-4 minutes until
browned on all sides, adding a little more oil
if necessary. Push pork to one side and add
onion, garlic and ginger and stir-fry for 1
minute, tossing all the ingredients.

Add sambal oelek or chilli sauce, soy sauce
and 150 ml (5 fl oz/⅔ cup) water; stir. Bring
to the boil, then reduce heat to low and
simmer gently, covered, for 20-25 minutes,
stirring occasionally, until pork is tender and
sauce thickened. Garnish with coriander and
serve with fried rice or noodles.

Serves 4.

Note: Sambal oelek is a very hot, chilli-based
Indonesian condiment available in specialist
or oriental food shops.

BARBECUED PORK

750 g (1½ lb) pork loin, cut into long strips
115 g (4 oz/⅔ cup) brown sugar
3 tablespoons boiling water
1 tablespoon dark soy sauce
1 tablespoon oyster sauce
2 tablespoons rice wine or dry sherry
1 teaspoon sesame oil
½ teaspoon sea salt
½ teaspoon edible red food colouring, if desired
Chinese shredded lettuce, to serve

Place pork in a medium bowl. In a small bowl, stir together sugar and boiling water until sugar dissolves, then stir in remaining ingredients. Cool slightly, then pour over pork, turning pork several times to coat evenly. Leave for 8 hours turning the pork several times. Lift pork from marinade, allowing excess to drain off, reserve. Preheat barbecue or grill.

Thread meat onto meat skewers and barbecue or grill for about 8 minutes until crisp and cooked, basting several times with reserved marinade. To serve, remove the pork from the skewers, cut into bite-sized pieces and serve on a bed of shredded Chinese lettuce.

Serves 4-6.

CHINESE SAUSAGE STIR-FRY

2 tablespoons sesame or vegetable oil
225 g (8 oz) Chinese sausage (see Note) or sweet
    Italian-style sausage, cut diagonally into thin slices
1 onion, cut in half lengthwise and sliced
1 red pepper (capsicum), diced
115 g (4 oz) baby sweetcorn
2 courgettes (zucchini), thinly sliced
115 g (4 oz) mange tout (snow peas)
8 spring onions, cut into 2.5 cm (1 in) pieces
25 g (1 oz) beansprouts, rinsed and drained
25 g (1 oz/¼ cup) cashew nuts or peanuts
2 tablespoons soy sauce
3 tablespoons dry sherry or rice wine

Heat the wok until hot. Add sesame or vegetable oil and swirl to coat wok. Add sausage slices and stir-fry for 3-4 minutes until browned and cooked. Add onion, pepper and sweetcorn and stir-fry for 3 minutes. Add courgettes (zucchini), mange tout (snow peas) and spring onions and stir-fry for a further 2 minutes.

Stir in the beansprouts and nuts and stir-fry for 1-2 minutes. Add soy sauce and dry sherry or rice wine and stir-fry for 1 minute until vegetables are tender but still crisp and sausage slices completely cooked through. Serve with rice or noodles.

Serve 4.

Note: Chinese sausage is available in Chinese groceries and some specialist shops and needs cooking before being used.

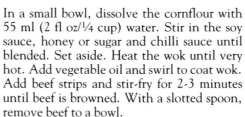

TERIYAKI STEAKS

55 ml (2 fl oz/¼ cup) mirin or dry sherry sweetened
  with 1 teaspoon sugar
55 ml (2 fl oz/¼ cup) light soy sauce
1 cm (½ in) piece fresh root ginger, peeled and minced
1 clove garlic, finely chopped
1 teaspoon sugar
½ teaspoon red pepper sauce (or to taste)
4 sirloin or fillet steaks, cut into strips
2 tablespoons sesame oil
4 spring onions, thinly sliced
fresh coriander leaves, to garnish

In a shallow baking dish, combine mirin or
sweetened dry sherry, soy sauce, ginger,
garlic, sugar and red pepper sauce to taste.

Add the steak strips and turn to coat well.
Leave to stand for 1 hour, turning strips once
or twice.

Heat the wok until very hot. Add sesame oil
and swirl to coat. Drain meat, reserving marinade, and add to wok. Stir-fry for 2-3 minutes
until browned on all sides. Pour over marinade and add spring onions. Cook for 3-5
minutes until steaks are cooked to desired
doneness and most of marinade has evaporated, glazing the meat. Garnish with coriander
leaves and serve with marinated cucumber or
daikon (mooli) salad and rice.

Serves 4.

CHILLI BEEF WITH PEPPERS

1 tablespoon cornflour
55 ml (2 fl oz/¼ cup) light soy sauce
1 tablespoon honey or brown sugar
1 teaspoon Chinese chilli sauce
2 tablespoons vegetable oil
450 g (1 lb) rump or sirloin steak, cut crosswise into
  thin strips
1 tablespoon sesame oil
2 cloves garlic, finely chopped
1 chilli, seeded and thinly sliced
1 onion, thinly sliced
1 red pepper (capsicum), cut into thin strips
1 green pepper (capsicum), cut into thin strips
1 yellow pepper (capsicum), cut into thin strips

In a small bowl, dissolve the cornflour with
55 ml (2 fl oz/¼ cup) water. Stir in the soy
sauce, honey or sugar and chilli sauce until
blended. Set aside. Heat the wok until very
hot. Add vegetable oil and swirl to coat wok.
Add beef strips and stir-fry for 2-3 minutes
until beef is browned. With a slotted spoon,
remove beef to a bowl.

Add sesame oil to the wok and add garlic and
chilli. Stir-fry for 1 minute until fragrant.
Add onion and pepper (capsicum) strips and
stir-fry for 2-3 minutes until beginning to
soften. Stir cornflour mixture, then stir into
wok and stir until sauce bubbles and begins to
thicken. Add beef strips and any juices and
stir-fry for 1 minute until beef is heated
through. Serve with rice.

Serves 4.

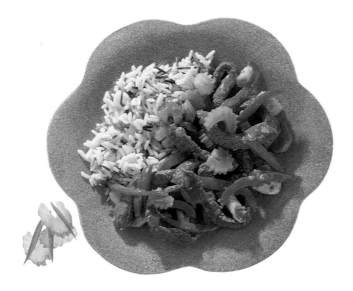

BEEF IN OYSTER SAUCE

DRY-FRIED BEEF STRIPS

3 teaspoons cornflour
1½ tablespoons soy sauce
1½ tablespoons rice wine or dry sherry
450 g (1 lb) rump, sirloin or fillet steak, cut crosswise
    into thin strips
2 tablespoons sesame oil
1 cm (½ in) piece fresh root ginger, peeled and chopped
2 cloves garlic, finely chopped
4 stalks celery, sliced
1 red pepper (capsicum), sliced
115 g (4 oz) mushrooms, sliced
4 spring onions, sliced
2 tablespoons oyster sauce
115 ml (4 fl oz/½ cup) chicken stock or water

2 tablespoons sesame oil
450 g (1 lb) rump or sirloin steak, cut crosswise
    into julienne strips
2 tablespoons rice wine or dry sherry
1 tablespoon light soy sauce
2 cloves garlic, finely chopped
1 cm (½ in) piece fresh root ginger, peeled and
    finely chopped
1 tablespoon Chinese chilli bean paste (sauce)
2 teaspoons sugar
1 carrot, peeled and cut into julienne strips
2 stalks celery, cut into julienne strips
2-3 spring onions, thinly sliced
¼ teaspoon ground Szechuan pepper
cucumber matchsticks, to garnish

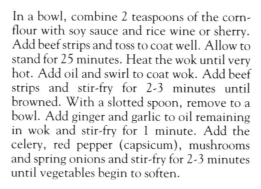

In a bowl, combine 2 teaspoons of the corn-flour with soy sauce and rice wine or sherry. Add beef strips and toss to coat well. Allow to stand for 25 minutes. Heat the wok until very hot. Add oil and swirl to coat wok. Add beef strips and stir-fry for 2-3 minutes until browned. With a slotted spoon, remove to a bowl. Add ginger and garlic to oil remaining in wok and stir-fry for 1 minute. Add the celery, red pepper (capsicum), mushrooms and spring onions and stir-fry for 2-3 minutes until vegetables begin to soften.

Heat the wok until very hot. Add the oil and swirl to coat wok. Add beef and stir-fry for 15 seconds to quickly seal meat. Add 1 table-spoon rice wine or sherry and stir-fry for 1-2 minutes until beef is browned. Pour off and reserve any excess liquid and continue stir-frying until beef is dry.

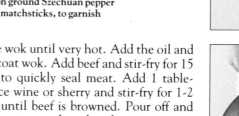

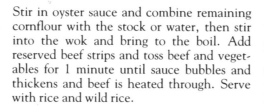

Stir in oyster sauce and combine remaining cornflour with the stock or water, then stir into the wok and bring to the boil. Add reserved beef strips and toss beef and vegetables for 1 minute until sauce bubbles and thickens and beef is heated through. Serve with rice and wild rice.

Serves 4.

Stir in soy sauce, garlic, ginger, chilli bean paste, sugar, remaining rice wine or sherry and any reserved cooking juices and stir to blend well. Add carrot, celery, spring onions and ground Szechuan pepper and stir-fry until the vegetables begin to soften and all the liquid is absorbed. Garnish with cucumber matchsticks and serve with rice and wild rice.

Serves 4.

—THAI BEEF WITH NOODLES— | —SPICY SESAME BEEF—

55 ml (2 fl oz/¼ cup) rice wine or dry sherry
2 tablespoons light soy sauce
2 cloves garlic, finely chopped
2.5 cm (1 in) piece fresh root ginger, peeled and
  finely chopped
½ teaspoon dried crushed chillies
450 g (1 lb) sirloin or fillet steak, 2.5 cm (1 in) thick,
  cut crosswise into 1 cm (½ in) strips
350 g (12 oz) ramen noodles or thin spaghetti
1 tablespoon sesame oil
115 g (4 oz) mange tout (snow peas)
4-6 spring onions, cut into 5 cm (2 in) pieces
2 teaspoons cornflour dissolved in 55 ml
  (2 fl oz/¼ cup) water
2 tablespoons chopped fresh coriander
fresh coriander leaves and lime slices, to garnish

1 tablespoon cornflour
3 tablespoons light soy sauce
450 g (1 lb) rump, sirloin or fillet steak, cut crosswise
  into thin strips
350 g (12 oz) broccoli
2 tablespoons sesame oil
2.5 cm (1 in) piece fresh root ginger, peeled and cut into
  julienne strips
2 cloves garlic, finely chopped
1 fresh chilli, seeded and thinly sliced
1 red pepper (capsicum), thinly sliced
400 g (14 oz) baby corn
115 ml (4 fl oz/½ cup) beef or chicken stock, or water
4-6 spring onions, cut into 5 cm (2 in) pieces
toasted sesame seeds, to garnish

In a shallow baking dish, combine wine or sherry, soy sauce, garlic, ginger and chillies. Add steak, cover and leave to marinate for 30 minutes, turning once. Cook noodles or spaghetti according to packet directions, rinse, drain and set aside. Heat wok until very hot. Add sesame oil and swirl to coat wok. Remove steak from marinade, scraping off any ginger and garlic and reserving marinade. Pat steak dry with absorbent kitchen paper. Add steak to wok and stir-fry for 4-5 minutes, until browned on all sides. Remove and keep warm.

In a bowl, combine cornflour and soy sauce. Add beef strips and toss to coat well. Leave to stand for 20 minutes. Cut large flowerets from the broccoli and divide into small flowerets. With a swivel-bladed vegetable peeler, peel the stalk and cut diagonally into 2.5 cm (1 in) pieces. Heat the wok until very hot. Add sesame oil and swirl to coat. Add beef strips and marinade and stir-fry for 2-3 minutes until browned.

Add mange tout (snow peas) and spring onions to any oil remaining in wok and stir-fry for 1 minute. Stir cornflour mixture and stir into wok with reserved marinade and bring to the boil. Add reserved noodles and beef and chopped coriander. Toss to coat well. Divide among 4 plates. Garnish with coriander leaves and lime slices.

Serves 4.

With a slotted spoon, remove beef strips to a bowl. Add ginger, garlic and chilli to the wok and stir-fry for 1 minute. Add broccoli, red pepper (capsicum) and baby corn and stir-fry for 2-3 minutes until broccoli is tender but still crisp. Add the stock and stir for 1 minute until sauce bubbles and thickens. Add spring onions and reserved beef strips and stir-fry for 1-2 minutes until beef strips are heated through. Sprinkle with sesame seeds and serve with rice or noodles.

Serves 4.

RICE & NOODLES

EGG FRIED RICE

150 g (5 oz) long-grain rice
3 eggs, beaten
2 tablespoons vegetable oil
1 clove garlic, finely chopped
3 spring onions (scallions), finely chopped
115 g (4 oz) cooked peas, or frozen, thawed
1 tablespoon light soy sauce
1 teaspoon sea salt

Cook rice in plenty of boiling water for 15 minutes until tender but still firm to the bite. Drain and rinse with boiling water. In a small saucepan, cook eggs over a moderately low heat, stirring until lightly scrambled. Remove and keep warm.

In a wok, heat oil, add garlic, spring onions (scallions) and peas and stir-fry for 1 minute. Stir in rice to mix thoroughly.

Add soy sauce, eggs and salt. Stir to break up egg and mix thoroughly.

Serves 4.

GREEN FRIED RICE

150 g (5 oz) long-grain rice
3 eggs, beaten
4 tablespoons vegetable oil
225 g (8 oz) spring greens, ribs removed and finely sliced
1 clove garlic, finely chopped
4 spring onions (scallions), finely chopped
115 g (4 oz) ham, shredded

Cook rice in plenty of boiling water for 15 minutes until tender but still firm to the bite. Drain and rinse with boiling water. Use eggs to make an omelette, then cut it into thin strips.

In a wok, heat 1 tablespoon vegetable oil, add greens and fry for 1 minute; remove and keep warm.

Add remaining oil to the work, add garlic and spring onions (scallions) and stir-fry for 1 minute, then stir in the rice. When mixed thoroughly, stir in ham, greens, omelette slices and salt.

Serves 4.

CRAB FRIED RICE

YANGCHOW FRIED RICE

150 g (5 oz) long-grain rice
3 eggs, beaten
85 g (3 oz) can crab meat
2 tablespoons vegetable oil
175 g (6 oz) beansprouts
1 tablespoon light soy sauce
6 spring onions (scallions), finely chopped
1 teaspoon sesame oil

Cook rice in plenty of boiling water for 15 minutes until tender but still firm to the bite. Drain and rinse with boiling water. In a bowl mix together eggs and crab meat with its liquid. Use to make an omelette, then cut it into strips.

150 g (5 oz) long-grain rice
3 tablespoons peanut oil
2 medium onions, finely sliced
3 slices fresh root ginger, peeled and finely chopped
115 g (4 oz) pork tenderloin, minced
1 tablespoon light soy sauce
1 teaspoon brown sugar
½ teaspoon sea salt
2 eggs, beaten
3 dried black winter mushrooms, soaked in hot water for 25 minutes, drained and squeezed
2 large tomatoes, peeled, seeded and chopped
55 g (2 oz) cooked peas, or frozen peas, thawed

In a wok, heat vegetable oil, add beansprouts and fry for 1 minute. Remove from wok and keep warm.

Cook rice in plenty of boiling water for 15 minutes until tender but still firm to the bite. Drain and rinse with boiling water. In a wok, heat oil, add onion and ginger and stir-fry for 2 minutes. Stir in pork, continue stirring for 3 minutes until crisp then add soy sauce and sugar. Stir-fry for 1 minute, then stir in rice. Remove to a warmed dish and keep warm.

Add rice to wok and stir-fry for 3 mintues. Stir in soy sauce and cook for a further 2 minutes. Stir in beansprouts, omelette strips and spring onions (scallions), and cook for 2-3 minutes. Serve sprinkled with sesame oil.

Serves 4.

Pour eggs into wok, season with salt and pepper, then cook stirring for 2-3 minutes until just beginning to set. Stir in mushrooms, tomatoes and peas. Cook for 2-3 minutes, then stir in rice mixture.

Serves 4.

THAI FRIED RICE

SPICY FRIED RICE

175 g (6 oz/¾ cup) long-grain white rice
115 g (4 oz) long beans, or French beans, cut into
   2.5 cm (1 in) lengths
3 tablespoons vegetable oil
2 onions, finely chopped
3 cloves garlic, crushed
85 g (3 oz) lean pork, very finely chopped
85 g (3 oz) chicken breast meat, very finely chopped
2 eggs, beaten
2 tablespoons Nam Prik, see page 19
1 tablespoon fish sauce
85 g (3 oz) cooked peeled prawns
coriander leaves, sliced spring onions (scallions) and
   lime wedges, to garnish

175 g (6 oz/¾ cup) long-grain white rice
2 tablespoons vegetable oil
1 large onion, finely chopped
3 cloves garlic, chopped
2 fresh green chillies, seeded and finely chopped
2 tablespoons Red Curry Paste, see page 18
55 g (2 oz) lean pork, very finely chopped
3 eggs, beaten
1 tablespoon fish sauce
55 g (2 oz) cooked peeled prawns
finely sliced red chilli, shredded coriander leaves and
   Spring Onion (Scallion) Brushes (see page 15),
   to garnish

Cook rice, see page 12. Add beans to a saucepan of boiling water and cook for 2 minutes. Drain and refresh under cold running water. Drain well. In a wok, heat oil, add onions and garlic and cook, stirring occasionally, until softened. Stir in pork and chicken and stir-fry for 1 minute. Push to side of wok.

Cook rice, see page 12. In a wok, heat oil, add onion, garlic and chillies and cook, stirring occasionally, until onion has softened. Stir in curry paste and continue to stir for 3-4 minutes. Add pork and stir-fry for 2-3 minutes. Stir in rice to coat with ingredients, then push to sides of wok.

Pour eggs into centre of wok, leave until just beginning to set, then stir in pork mixture followed by nam prik, fish sauce and rice. Stir for 1-2 minutes, then add beans and prawns. Serve garnished with coriander leaves, spring onions (scallions) and lime wedges.

Serves 4.

Pour eggs into centre of wok. When just beginning to set, mix evenly into the rice, adding fish sauce at the same time. Stir in prawns, then transfer to a shallow, warmed serving dish. Garnish with chilli, coriander and spring onion (scallion) brushes.

Serves 4.

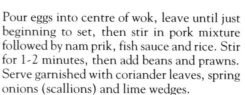

THAI RICE NOODLES

225 g (8 oz) flat rice noodles
3 tablespoons vegetable oil
2 cloves garlic, peeled and chopped
1 red pepper (capsicum), thinly sliced
1 tablespoon soy sauce
1 teaspoon chilli sauce
6 teaspoons nam pla (fish sauce)
4 teaspoons wine vinegar
1 tablespoon brown sugar
450 g (1 lb) cooked peeled prawns, defrosted if frozen
    and patted dry
175 g (6 oz) beansprouts, trimmed and rinsed
6 spring onions, thinly sliced
4 tablespoons sesame oil
3 tablespoons chopped peanuts, to garnish

Place the rice noodles in a large, heatproof bowl. Pour over enough hot water to cover noodles by 5 cm (2 in) and leave to stand for 15-20 minutes until softened. Drain and set aside. Heat the wok until hot. Add the oil and swirl to coat wok. Add garlic and red pepper (capsicum) and stir-fry for 2-3 minutes until pepper is tender but still crisp. Add noodles, soy sauce, chilli sauce, nam pla (fish sauce), vinegar and brown sugar and stir-fry for 1 minute. Add a little water if noodles begin to stick.

Stir in prawns, beansprouts, spring onions and sesame oil and stir-fry for 2-3 minutes until prawns are heated through. Sprinkle with peanuts and serve hot.

Serves 4.

CHICKEN & MUSHROOM RICE

175 g (6 oz/¾ cup) long-grain white rice
2 tablespoons vegetable oil
1 small onion, finely chopped
2 cloves garlic, finely chopped
2 fresh red chillies, seeded and cut into slivers
225 g (8 oz) chicken breast meat, finely chopped
85 g (3 oz) bamboo shoots, chopped or cut into
    matchstick strips
8 pieces dried Chinese black mushrooms, soaked for 30
    minutes, drained and chopped
2 tablespoons dried shrimps
1 tablespoon fish sauce
about 25 Thai holy basil leaves
Thai holy basil sprig, to garnish

Cook rice, see page 12. In a wok, heat oil, add onion and garlic and cook, stirring occasionally, until golden. Add chillies and chicken and stir-fry for 2 minutes.

Stir in bamboo shoots, mushrooms, dried shrimps and fish sauce. Continue to stir for 2 minutes, then stir in rice and basil. Serve garnished with basil sprig.

Serves 4.

COCONUT NOODLES

NOODLES & THAI HERB SAUCE

225 g (8 oz) wholewheat linguine, tagliatelle
 or spaghetti
55 ml (2 fl oz/¼ cup) groundnut oil
115 g (4 oz) shiitake or oyster mushrooms
1 red pepper (capsicum), thinly sliced
½ small Chinese cabbage, thinly shredded
115 g (4 oz) mange tout (snow peas), thinly sliced
4-6 spring onions, thinly sliced
175 ml (6 fl oz/¾ cup) unsweetened coconut milk
2 tablespoons rice wine or dry sherry
1 tablespoon soy sauce
1 tablespoon oyster sauce
1 teaspoon Chinese chilli sauce
3 teaspoons cornflour dissolved in 2 tablespoons water
8 tablespoons chopped fresh mint or coriander
mint or coriander sprigs, to garnish

75 ml (2½ fl oz/⅓ cup) vegetable oil
2 tablespoons raw shelled peanuts
1 small fresh green chilli, seeded and sliced
2 cm (¾ in) piece galangal, chopped
2 large cloves garlic, chopped
leaves from bunch Thai holy basil (about 90)
leaves from small bunch Thai mint (about 30)
leaves from small bunch coriander (about 45)
2 tablespoons lime juice
1 teaspoon fish sauce
350-450 g (12-16 oz) egg noodles, soaked for
 5-10 minutes

In a large saucepan of boiling water, cook the noodles according to the packet directions. Drain and toss with 1 tablespoon of ground-nut oil. Heat the wok until hot. Add the remaining oil and swirl to coat wok. Add mushrooms, pepper (capsicum) and Chinese cabbage and stir-fry for 2-3 minutes until vegetables begin to soften. Stir in reserved noodles, mange tout (snow peas) and spring onions and stir-fry for 1 minute to combine.

Over a high heat, heat oil in a wok, add peanuts and cook, stirring, for about 2 minutes until browned. Using a slotted spoon, transfer nuts to absorbent kitchen paper to drain; reserve oil.

Slowly pour in coconut milk, rice wine or sherry, soy sauce, oyster sauce and chilli sauce and bring to simmering point. Stir the cornflour mixture and, pushing ingredients to one side, stir into the wok. Stir to combine liquid ingredients well, then stir in chopped mint or coriander and toss to coat well. Stir-fry for 2-3 minutes until heated through. Serve hot, garnished with sprigs of mint or coriander.

Serves 4.

Using a small blender, roughly grind nuts. Add chilli, galangal and garlic. Mix briefly. Add herbs, lime juice, fish sauce and reserved oil. Drain noodles, shake loose, then cook in a pan of boiling salted water for 2 minutes until soft. Drain well, turn into a warmed dish and toss with sauce.

Serves 4.

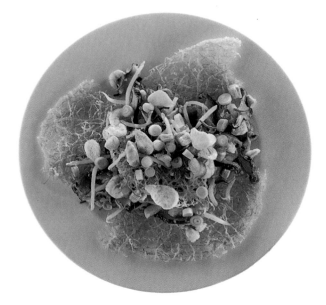

CRISPY NOODLES

175 g (6 oz) rice vermicelli
6 pieces dried Chinese black mushrooms
115 g (4 oz) lean pork
115 g (4 oz) chicken breast
vegetable oil for deep frying
2 eggs
4 cloves garlic, finely chopped
3 shallots, thinly sliced
1 fresh red chilli, seeded and sliced
1 fresh green chilli, seeded and sliced
6 tablespoons lime juice
1 tablespoon fish sauce
1 tablespoon crushed palm sugar
45 g (1½ oz) cooked peeled shrimps
115 g (4 oz) beansprouts
3 spring onions (scallions), thickly sliced

Add more oil to wok until there is sufficient for deep frying. Heat to 190C (375F). Add vermicelli in batches and fry until puffed, light golden brown and crisp. Transfer to absorbent kitchen paper. Set aside.

Soak vermicelli in water for 20 minutes, then drain and set aside. Soak mushrooms in water for 20 minutes, then drain, chop and set aside. Cut pork and chicken into 2.5 cm (1 in) strips or small dice. Set aside.

Pour off oil leaving 3 tablespoons. Add garlic and shallots and cook, stirring occasionally, until lightly browned. Add pork, stir-fry for 1 minute, then mix in chicken and stir for 2 minutes. Stir in chillies, mushrooms, lime juice, fish sauce and sugar.

For garnish, heat 2 teaspoons oil in a wok. In a small bowl, beat eggs with 2 tablespoons water, then drip small amounts in batches in tear shapes onto wok. Cook for 1½-2 minutes until set. Remove using a fish slice or thin spatula. Set aside.

Bubble until liquid becomes very lightly syrupy. Add shrimps, beansprouts and noodles, tossing to coat with sauce without breaking up noodles. Serve with spring onions (scallions) scattered over and garnished with egg 'tears'.

Serves 4.

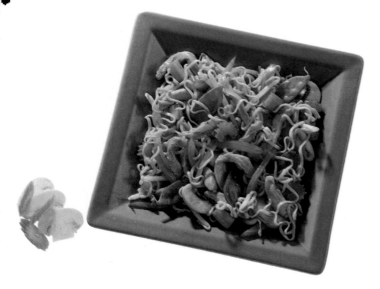

CHOW MIEN

3 tablespoons soy sauce
2 tablespoons dry sherry or rice wine
1 teaspoon Chinese chilli paste or sauce
1 tablespoon sesame oil
6 teaspoons cornflour
350 g (12 oz) skinned and boned chicken breasts, cut into shreds
225 g (8 oz) Chinese long egg noodles or linguine
2 tablespoons vegetable oil
2 stalks celery, thinly sliced
175 g (6 oz) mushrooms
1 red or green pepper (capsicum), thinly sliced
115 g (4 oz) mange tout (snow peas)
4-6 spring onions
115 ml (4 fl oz/½ cup) chicken stock or water
115 g (4 oz) beansprouts, trimmed and rinsed

In a shallow baking dish, combine the soy sauce, sherry or rice wine, chilli paste or sauce, sesame oil and cornflour. Add the shredded chicken and toss to coat evenly. Allow to stand 20 minutes. In a large saucepan of boiling water, cook the egg noodles or linguine according to the packet directions. Drain and set aside.

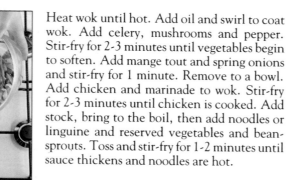

Heat wok until hot. Add oil and swirl to coat wok. Add celery, mushrooms and pepper. Stir-fry for 2-3 minutes until vegetables begin to soften. Add mange tout and spring onions and stir-fry for 1 minute. Remove to a bowl. Add chicken and marinade to wok. Stir-fry for 2-3 minutes until chicken is cooked. Add stock, bring to the boil, then add noodles or linguine and reserved vegetables and beansprouts. Toss and stir-fry for 1-2 minutes until sauce thickens and noodles are hot.

Serves 4-6.

SINGAPORE NOODLES

225 g (8 oz) thin round egg noodles
55 ml (2 fl oz/¼ cup) vegetable oil
2 cloves garlic, chopped
2.5 cm (1 in) piece fresh root ginger, peeled and finely chopped
1 fresh chilli, seeded and chopped
1 red pepper (capsicum), thinly sliced
115 g (4 oz) mange tout (snow peas), sliced if large
4-6 spring onions, finely sliced
175 g (6 oz) peeled cooked prawns, defrosted if frozen
115 g (4 oz) beansprouts, trimmed, rinsed and dried
70 ml (2½ fl oz/⅓ cup) tomato ketchup (sauce)
1 teaspoon chilli powder
1-2 teaspoons chilli sauce

In a large saucepan of boiling water, cook the noodles according to packet directions. Drain and toss with 1 tablespoon of the oil. Set aside. Heat the wok until hot. Add remaining oil and swirl to coat the wok. Add garlic, ginger and chilli and stir-fry for 1 minute. Add red pepper (capsicum) and mange tout (snow peas) and stir-fry for 1 minute.

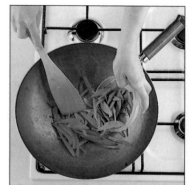

Add spring onions, prawns and beansprouts and stir in the tomato ketchup (sauce), chilli powder, chilli sauce and 115 ml (4 fl oz/½ cup) water. Bring to the boil. Add noodles and toss. Stir-fry for 1-2 minutes until coated with sauce and heated through. Turn into large shallow serving bowl and serve at once.

Serves 4.

VEGETARIAN DISHES & SALADS

SZECHUAN AUBERGINE

STIR-FRIED MANGE TOUT

450 g (1 lb) small aubergines (eggplants), cut into
   2.5 cm (1 in) cubes or thin slices
salt
2 tablespoons groundnut oil
2 cloves garlic, finely chopped
2.5 cm (1 in) piece fresh root ginger, peeled and
   finely chopped
3-4 spring onions, finely sliced
2 tablespoons dark soy sauce
3-6 teaspoons chilli bean paste or sauce or 1 teaspoon
   crushed dried chillies
1 tablespoon yellow bean paste (optional)
2 tablespoons dry sherry or rice wine
3 teaspoons cider vinegar
1 tablespoon sugar
chopped fresh parsley, to garnish

2 tablespoons vegetable oil
3 cloves garlic, finely chopped
115 g (4 oz) lean pork, very finely chopped
450 g (1 lb) mange tout (snow peas)
½ teaspoon crushed palm sugar
1 tablespoon fish sauce
55 g (2 oz) cooked peeled prawns, chopped
freshly ground black pepper

In a wok, heat oil over a medium heat, add
garlic and fry until lightly coloured. Add pork
and stir-fry for 2-3 minutes.

Place aubergine (eggplant) cubes in a plastic
or stainless steel colander or sieve, placed on
a plate or baking sheet. Sprinkle with salt and
leave to stand 30 minutes. Rinse aubergine
(eggplant) under cold running water and turn
out onto layers of absorbent kitchen paper;
pat dry thoroughly. Heat wok until very hot.
Add oil and swirl to coat wok. Add garlic,
ginger and spring onions and stir-fry for
1-2 minutes until spring onions begin to
soften. Add aubergine (eggplant) and stir-fry
for 2-3 minutes until softened and beginning
to brown.

Add mange tout (snow peas) and stir-fry for
about 3 minutes until cooked but still crisp.

Stir in remaining ingredients and 150 ml
(5 fl oz/⅔ cup) water and bring to the boil.
Reduce the heat and simmer for 5-7 minutes
until aubergine (eggplant) is very tender, stirring frequently. Increase heat to high and
stir-fry mixture until the liquid is almost
completely reduced. Spoon into serving dish
and garnish with parsley.

Serves 4-6.

Stir in sugar, fish sauce, prawns and black
pepper. Heat briefly and serve.

Serves 4-6.

TOSSED GREENS

SPICED CABBAGE

2 tablespoons peanut oil
225 g (8 oz) chicken breast meat, very finely chopped
6 cloves garlic, finely chopped
700 g (1½ lb) spinach leaves, torn into large pieces if
   necessary
1½ tablespoons fish sauce
freshly ground black pepper
1½ tablespoons dry-fried unsalted peanuts, chopped
thinly sliced fresh seeded chilli, to garnish

In a wok, heat oil, add chicken and stir-fry for
2-3 minutes. Using a slotted spoon, transfer
to absorbent kitchen paper; set aside.

14 black peppercorns
2 tablespoons coconut cream, see page 10
2 shallots, chopped
115 g (4 oz) lean pork, very finely chopped
about 450 g (1 lb) white cabbage, finely sliced
315 ml (10 fl oz/1¼ cups) coconut milk
1 tablespoon fish sauce
1 fresh red chilli, seeded and very finely chopped

In a wok, heat peppercorns for about 3
minutes until aroma changes. Stir in coconut
cream, heat for 2-3 minutes, then stir in
shallots.

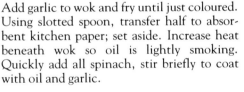

Add garlic to wok and fry until just coloured.
Using slotted spoon, transfer half to absorbent kitchen paper; set aside. Increase heat
beneath wok so oil is lightly smoking.
Quickly add all spinach, stir briefly to coat
with oil and garlic.

Stir-fry for a further 2-3 minutes, then stir in
pork and cabbage. Cook, stirring occasionally, for 3 minutes, then add coconut milk
and bring just to the boil. Cover and simmer
for 5 minutes.

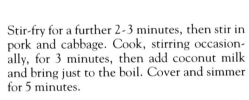

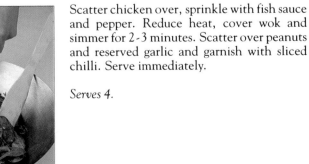

Scatter chicken over, sprinkle with fish sauce
and pepper. Reduce heat, cover wok and
simmer for 2-3 minutes. Scatter over peanuts
and reserved garlic and garnish with sliced
chilli. Serve immediately.

Serves 4.

Uncover and cook for about 10 minutes until
cabbage is tender but retains some bite. Stir
in fish sauce. Serve sprinkled with chilli.

Serves 4-5.

—VEGETABLES WITH SAUCE— MUSHROOMS & BEANSPROUTS

1 aubergine (eggplant), about 225 g (8 oz)
115 g (4 oz) long beans or green beans
85 g (3 oz) cauliflower flowerets
500 ml (16 fl oz/2 cups) coconut milk
2 red shallots, chopped
2 cloves garlic, chopped
4 coriander roots, chopped
2 dried red chillies, seeded and chopped
1 stalk lemon grass, chopped
3 cm (1¼ in) piece galangal, chopped
grated peel 1 kaffir lime
4 tablespoons coconut cream, see page 10
1½ tablespoons ground roasted peanuts
3 tablespoons tamarind water, see page 12
1 tablespoon fish sauce
2 teaspoons crushed palm sugar

2 tablespoons vegetable oil
2 fresh red chillies, seeded and thinly sliced
2 cloves garlic, chopped
225 g (8 oz) shiitake mushrooms, sliced
115 g (4 oz) beansprouts
115 g (4 oz) cooked peeled prawns
2 tablespoons lime juice
2 red shallots, sliced into rings
1 tablespoon fish sauce
½ teaspoon crushed palm sugar
1 tablespoon ground browned rice, see page 12
6 coriander sprigs, stalks and leaves finely chopped
10 Thai mint leaves, shredded
Thai mint leaves, to garnish

Cut aubergine (eggplant) into 4 cm (1½ in) cubes; cut beans into 5 cm (2 in) lengths. Put aubergine (eggplant), beans and cauliflower into a saucepan, add coconut milk and bring to the boil. Cover and simmer for 10 minutes until vegetables are tender. Remove from heat, uncover and set aside. Using a pestle and mortar or small blender, pound or mix together shallots, garlic, coriander roots, chillies, lemon grass, galangal and lime peel.

In a wok, heat oil, add chillies and garlic and cook, stirring occasionally, for 2-3 minutes. Add mushrooms and stir-fry for 2-3 minutes.

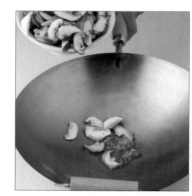

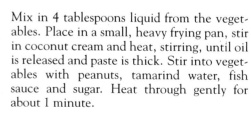

Mix in 4 tablespoons liquid from the vegetables. Place in a small, heavy frying pan, stir in coconut cream and heat, stirring, until oil is released and paste is thick. Stir into vegetables with peanuts, tamarind water, fish sauce and sugar. Heat through gently for about 1 minute.

Serves 6.

Add beansprouts and prawns, stir-fry for 1 minute, then stir in lime juice, shallots, fish sauce and sugar. When hot, remove from heat and stir in rice, coriander and mint. Serve garnished with mint leaves.

Serves 4.

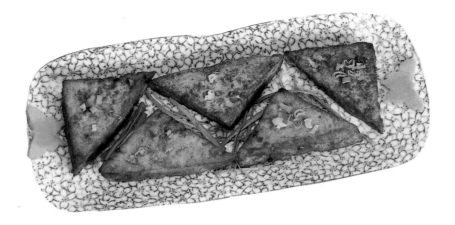

DEEP-FRIED TOFU

1 tablespoon sea salt
1 tablespoon Chinese five-spice powder
2 tablespoons granulated sugar
1 teaspoon ground white pepper
1 clove garlic, very finely chopped
4 cakes tofu, halved
625 ml (20 fl oz/2½ cups) peanut oil
4 spring onions (scallions), very finely chopped

In a bowl, mix together salt, five-spice powder, sugar, pepper and garlic. Add one piece of tofu at a time and turn over to evenly coat. Leave for 1 hour.

In a wok, heat oil until smoking, add tofu and deep-fry for 5 minutes until puffy and golden. Drain on absorbent kitchen paper.

Serve immediately sprinkled with the spring onions (scallions).

Serves 4.

CRISPY SEAWEED

875 g (1¾ lb) young spring (collard) greens
625 ml (20 fl oz/2½ cups) vegetable oil
1 tablespoon brown sugar
½ teaspoon sea salt
½ teaspoon ground cinnamon
85 g (3 oz/¾ cup) flaked almonds to garnish, if desired

Remove the thick ribs from the leaves and discard. Wash the leaves and drain and dry thoroughly with absorbent kitchen paper. Using a very sharp knife or cleaver cut the leaves into very fine shreds.

In a wok, heat the oil until smoking, then remove from heat and add greens. Return to a medium heat and stir for 2-3 minutes, or until the shreds begin to float. Using a slotted spoon remove from the oil and drain on absorbent kitchen paper.

In a small bowl, mix together sugar, salt and cinnamon. Place 'seaweed' on a dish and sprinkle with the sugar mixture. Serve cold garnished with flaked almonds, if desired.

Serves 4.

BROCCOLI WITH SHRIMPS

BRAISED BAMBOO SHOOTS

3 tablespoons peanut oil
4 cloves garlic, finely chopped
1 fresh red chilli, seeded and thinly sliced
450g (1 lb) trimmed broccoli, cut diagonally into 2.5
   cm (1 in) slices
115 g (4 oz) cooked peeled shrimps
1 tablespoon fish sauce
½ teaspoon crushed palm sugar
Chilli Flowers, see page 15, to garnish

In a wok, heat oil, add garlic and fry, stirring
occasionally, until just beginning to colour.
Add chilli and cook for 2 minutes.

55 g (2 oz/½ cup) cornflour (cornstarch)
375 g (12 oz) canned bamboo shoots
2 tablespoons vegetable oil
4 slices fresh root ginger, peeled
185 ml (6 fl oz/¾ cup) Chinese Chicken Stock,
   see page 22
1 tablespoon dark soy sauce
1 teaspoon rice wine or dry sherry
1 teaspoon brown sugar
½ small red pepper (capsicum), thinly sliced
½ small green pepper (capsicum), thinly sliced
½ teaspoon sesame oil

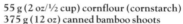

Quickly stir in broccoli. Stir-fry for 3
minutes. Reduce heat, cover wok and cook
for 4-5 minutes until broccoli is cooked but
still crisp.

Sieve cornflour (cornstarch) onto a plate,
toss in bamboo shoot slices to coat lightly and
evenly. Shake off excess. In a wok, heat
vegetable oil, add ginger, fry for 1 minute
then discard. Add bamboo shoots, stir-fry for
1 minute then stir in stock, soy sauce, rice
wine or dry sherry and sugar. Simmer for 5
minutes until bamboo shoots are just tender.

Remove lid, stir in shrimps, fish sauce and
sugar. Serve garnished with chilli flowers.

Serves 4.

Add peppers (capsicums) and cook for 3
minutes until softened. Sprinkle with sesame
oil before serving.

Serves 4.

SHANGHAI CASSEROLE

VEGETABLES IN A HAT

4 tablespoons peanut oil
175 g (6 oz) broccoli florets
175 g (6 oz) canned bamboo shoots, sliced
175 g (6 oz) carrot, thinly sliced
8 dried black winter mushrooms, soaked in hot water
   for 25 minutes, drained, liquid reserved
2 cakes tofu, cut into bite-sized pieces
2 teaspoons sea salt
1 teaspoon brown sugar
1 tablespoon dark soy sauce
2 tablespoons rice wine or dry sherry
1 teaspoon cornflour (cornstarch) dissolved in 2
   teaspoons water

4 tablespoons Chinese Chicken Stock, see page 22
1 tablespoon rice wine or dry sherry
½ teaspoon sea salt
¼ teaspoon granulated sugar
55 g (2 oz) dried wood ear mushrooms, soaked in hot
   water for 25 minutes, drained
4 dried black winter mushrooms, soaked in hot water
   for 25 minutes, drained
115 g (4 oz) beansprouts
85 g (3 oz) can bamboo shoots, drained and finely
   chopped
115 g (4 oz) Chinese cabbage, shredded
115 g (4 oz) bean thread noodles, soaked in hot water
   for 25 minutes, drained
2 eggs, beaten

In a saucepan, heat oil, add broccoli, bamboo shoots and carrot, and stir-fry for 3 minutes. Stir in mushrooms with their soaking liquid and remaining ingredients except cornflour (cornstarch) mixture and bring to the boil, stirring.

In a wok, bring chicken stock, rice wine or dry sherry, salt and sugar to the boil. Stir in mushrooms, beansprouts, bamboo shoots, cabbage and noodles, then simmer for 8 minutes. Drain vegetables and noodles, place in a warmed serving dish and keep warm.

Reduce heat so liquid simmers, cover and cook for 15 minutes. If there is too much liquid, stir in cornflour (cornstarch) mixture and heat, stirring until thickened.

Serves 4.

In a frying pan, use the eggs to make an omelette. Place the omelette on the vegetables and serve immediately.

Serves 4.

BEAN SALAD

2 tablespoons lime juice
2 tablespoons fish sauce
½ teaspoon crushed palm sugar
1½ tablespoons Nam Prik, see page 19
2 tablespoons ground roasted peanuts
2 tablespoons vegetable oil
3 cloves garlic, chopped
3 shallots, thinly sliced
¼ dried red chilli, seeded and finely chopped
2 tablespoons coconut cream, see page 10
225 g (8 oz) French beans, very thinly sliced

In a small bowl, mix together lime juice, fish sauce, sugar, nam prik, peanuts and 2 table-spoons water; set aside. In a small saucepan, heat oil, add garlic and shallots and cook, stirring occasionally, until beginning to brown. Stir in chilli and cook until garlic and shallots are browned. Using a slotted spoon, transfer to absorbent kitchen paper; set aside.

In a small saucepan over a low heat, warm coconut cream, stirring occasionally. Bring a saucepan of water to the boil, add beans, return to the boil and cook for about 30 seconds. Drain and refresh under cold running water. Drain well. Transfer to a serving bowl and toss with shallot mixture and contents of small bowl. Spoon over warm coconut cream.

Serves 3-4.

PRAWN SALAD WITH MINT

16-20 raw large prawns, peeled and deveined
juice 2 limes
2 teaspoons vegetable oil
2 teaspoons crushed palm sugar
2 tablespoons tamarind water, see page 12
1 tablespoon fish sauce
2 teaspoons Red Curry Paste, see page 18
2 stalks lemon grass, very finely chopped
4 tablespoons coconut cream, see page 10
10 Thai mint leaves, shredded
5 kaffir lime leaves, shredded
1 small crisp lettuce, divided into leaves
1 small cucumber, thinly sliced
Thai mint leaves, to garnish

Put prawns in a bowl, pour over lime juice and leave for 30 minutes. Remove prawns, allowing excess liquid to drain into bowl; reserve liquid. Heat oil in a wok, add prawns and stir-fry for 2-3 minutes until just cooked – marinating in lime juice partially cooks them.

Meanwhile, stir sugar, tamarind water, fish sauce, curry paste, lemon grass, coconut cream, mint and lime leaves into reserved lime liquid. Stir in cooked prawns. Set aside until cold. Make a bed of lettuce on a serving plate, place on a layer cucumber slices. Spoon prawns and dressing on top. Garnish with mint leaves.

Serves 3-4.

CHICKEN & WATERCRESS SALAD

2 cloves garlic, finely chopped
3 cm (1¼ in) piece galangal, finely chopped
1 tablespoon fish sauce
3 tablespoons lime juice
1 teaspoon crushed palm sugar
2 tablespoons peanut oil
225 g (8 oz) chicken breast meat, finely chopped
about 25 dried shrimps
1 bunch watercress, about 115 g (4 oz), coarse stalks
   removed
3 tablespoons chopped dry-roasted peanuts
2 fresh red chillies, seeded and cut into fine strips

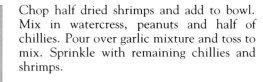

Using a pestle and mortar, pound together garlic and galangal. Mix in fish sauce, lime juice and sugar; set aside. In wok, heat oil, add chicken and stir-fry for about 3 minutes until cooked through. Using a slotted spoon, transfer to absorbent kitchen paper to drain. Put into a serving bowl and set aside.

Chop half dried shrimps and add to bowl. Mix in watercress, peanuts and half of chillies. Pour over garlic mixture and toss to mix. Sprinkle with remaining chillies and shrimps.

Serves 3-4.

CHILLI-CHICKEN SALAD

225 g (8 oz/1¼ cups) brown rice
3 tablespoons sesame oil
2 tablespoons peanut oil
150 g (5oz/1 cup) cashew nuts or peanuts
150 g (5 oz) mange tout (snow peas)
700 g (1½ lb) skinned and boned chicken breasts,
   cut into thin strips
2 tablespoons sunflower oil
2.5 cm (1 in) fresh ginger, peeled and thinly sliced
2 cloves garlic, finely chopped
4-6 spring onions, sliced
1-2 fresh green chillies, seeded and thinly sliced
3 tablespoons wine vinegar
2 tablespoons chopped fresh mint or coriander
mixed lettuce leaves
1 orange, peeled, segmented and any juice reserved

Cook rice for 30-35 minutes or according to directions, until tender. Drain and place in a large bowl; toss with sesame oil and set aside. Heat the wok until hot, add peanut oil and swirl to coat wok. Add the nuts and stir-fry for 1-2 minutes until they turn golden. Remove and add to rice. Add mange tout (snow peas) to oil in wok and stir-fry for 1-2 minutes until bright green. Add to the rice. Add chicken to the wok, in 2 batches, and stir-fry for 2-3 minutes until chicken turns white and feels firm to the touch. Add to the rice.

Add sunflower oil to wok and stir in ginger, garlic, spring onions and chillies. Stir-fry for 1 minute until onion begins to soften. Pour contents of wok over rice mixture. Return wok to heat and pour in vinegar, swirling to deglaze wok. Pour vinegar over rice mixture, add half the herbs and toss to mix well. Line a shallow serving bowl with lettuce. Spoon rice mixture on to leaves, decorate with orange segments and pour over any juice. Garnish with remaining herbs.

Serves 4.

THAI BEEF SALAD

PORK & BAMBOO SHOOT SALAD

350 g (12 oz) lean beef, very finely chopped
1 tablespoon fish sauce
2 tablespoons lime juice
2 teaspoons crushed palm sugar
1½ tablespoons long-grain white rice, browned and
    coarsely ground, see page 12
2 fresh green chillies, seeded and finely chopped
2 cloves garlic, finely chopped
8 Thai mint leaves
4 kaffir lime leaves, torn
8 Thai holy basil leaves
lettuce leaves, to serve
chopped spring onions (scallions) and a Chilli Flower,
    see page 15, to garnish

3 tablespoons vegetable oil
3 cloves garlic, chopped
1 small onion, thinly sliced
225 g (8 oz) lean pork, very finely chopped
1 egg, beaten
225 g (8 oz) can bamboo shoots, drained and cut
    into strips
1 tablespoon fish sauce
1 teaspoon crushed palm sugar
3 tablespoons lime juice
freshly ground black pepper
lettuce leaves, to serve

Heat a wok, add beef and dry-fry for about 2 minutes until tender. Transfer to a bowl. In a small bowl, mix together fish sauce, lime juice and sugar. Pour over warm beef, add rice and toss together. Cover and leave until cold.

In a wok, heat 2 tablespoons oil, add garlic and onion and cook, stirring occasionally, until lightly browned. Using a slotted spoon, transfer to absorbent kitchen paper to drain; set aside. Add pork to wok and stir-fry for about 3 minutes until cooked through. Using a slotted spoon, transfer to absorbent kitchen paper; set aside. Using absorbent kitchen paper, wipe out wok.

Add chillies, garlic, mint, lime and basil leaves to bowl and toss ingredients together. Line a plate with lettuce leaves and spoon beef mixture into centre. Scatter over spring onions (scallions) and garnish with a chilli flower.

Serves 3-4.

Heat remaining oil, pour in egg to make a thin layer and cook for 1-2 minutes until just set. Turn egg over and cook for 1 minute more. Remove egg from wok and roll up. Cut across into strips. In a bowl, toss together pork, bamboo shoots and egg. In a small bowl, stir together fish sauce, sugar, lime juice and pepper. Pour over pork mixture and toss. Serve on lettuce leaves and sprinkle with garlic and onion.

Serves 3-4.

DESSERTS

PEKING APPLES

CHINESE FRUIT SOUP

1 egg
125 ml (4 fl oz/½ cup) water
115 g (4 oz/1 cup) plain (all-purpose) flour
4 crisp eating apples
625 ml (20 fl oz/2½ cups) vegetable oil
SYRUP:
1 tablespoon vegetable oil
2 tablespoons water
6 tablespoons brown sugar
2 tablespoons golden syrup
iced water to set

In a large bowl, stir the egg and water into the flour to make a thick batter.

125 ml (4 fl oz/½ cup) rice wine or dry sherry
juice and rind of 2 limes
875 ml (28 fl oz/3½ cups) water
225 g (8 oz/1 cup) granulated sugar
1 piece lemon grass
4 whole cloves
5 cm (2 in) stick cinnamon
1 vanilla pod, split
pinch ground nutmeg
1 teaspoon coriander seeds, lightly crushed
45 g (1½ oz) piece fresh root ginger, peeled and thinly
    sliced
30 g (1 oz/¼ cup) raisins
500 g (1 lb) prepared sweet fruits, eg. mango,
    strawberries, lychees, star fruit, kiwi fruit

Peel, core and thickly slice apples. Dip each apple slice in the batter to evenly coat; allow excess to drain off. In a wok, heat oil until smoking. Add apple pieces in batches and deep-fry for 3 minutes until golden brown. Using a slotted spoon, remove to absorbent kitchen paper to drain.

In a saucepan, place rice wine or dry sherry, lime juice and rind, water, sugar, lemon grass, cloves, cinnamon, vanilla, nutmeg, coriander and ginger. Heat gently, stirring until sugar dissolves, then bring to the boil. Reduce heat and simmer for 5 minutes. Leave to cool, then strain into a bowl. Add raisins then chill.

To make syrup, in a small saucepan, gently heat oil, water and sugar, stirring until sugar has dissolved. Simmer for 5 minutes, stirring. Stir in golden syrup and boil for 5-10 minutes until hard and stringy. Reduce heat to very low. Dip each piece of apple into syrup to coat then place in ice cold water for a few seconds. Remove to a serving dish. Repeat with remaining apple. Serve immediately.

Serves 4.

Arrange a selection of prepared fruit in 4 individual serving dishes and spoon over syrup.

Serves 4.

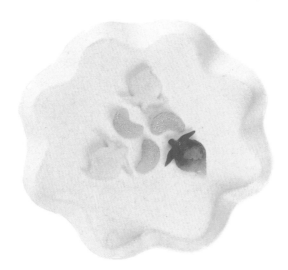

EXOTIC MANGO MOUSSE

COCONUT PANCAKES

440 g (14 oz) can mandarin segments, drained
440 g (14 oz) can mango pulp
440 ml (14 fl oz/1¾ cups) double (thick) cream
45 g (1½ oz) powdered gelatine
90 ml (3 fl oz/⅓ cup) water
4 egg whites
3 tablespoons brown sugar

Reserve a few mandarin segments. In a food processor or blender, process the remaining mandarins until smooth, pour into a measuring jug and add water to make 750 ml (24 fl oz/3 cups).

Turn into a large bowl; stir in mango pulp. In a bowl, whip cream until soft peaks form. Fold into mango mixture until just evenly combined. In a small bowl, sprinkle gelatine over water, leave to soften for 5 minutes then place bowl over a saucepan of boiling water. Stir until gelatine dissolves then remove bowl from heat and allow to cool slightly. Stir in a little of the mango mixture then stir into the large bowl; chill until almost set.

In a clean bowl, whisk egg whites until soft peaks form then whisk in sugar. Carefully fold into mango mixture until just evenly mixed. Serve in individual dishes decorated with the reserved mandarins.

Serves 8.

115 g (4 oz/⅔ cup) rice flour
85 g (3 oz/⅓ cup) caster sugar
pinch salt
85 g (3 oz/1 cup) desiccated coconut
2 eggs, beaten
625 ml (20 fl oz/2½ cups) coconut milk
green and red food colouring, if desired
vegetable oil for frying
mandarin segments, to serve, if desired

In a bowl, stir together rice flour, sugar, salt and coconut.

Form a well in centre, add egg, then gradually draw in flour, slowly pouring in coconut milk at same time, to make a smooth batter. If desired, divide batter evenly between 3 bowls. Stir green food colouring into one bowl to colour batter pale green; colour another batch pink and leave remaining batch plain. Heat a 15 cm (6 in) crêpe or omelette pan over a moderate heat, swirl around a little oil, then pour off excess. Stir batter well, then add 2-3 spoonfuls to pan.

Rotate to cover base, then cook over moderate heat for about 4 minutes until lightly browned underneath and quite firmly set. Carefully turn over and cook briefly on other side. Transfer to a warmed plate and keep warm while cooking remaining batter. Serve rolled up with mandarin segments, if liked.

Makes about 10.

Note: The mixture is quite delicate and the first few pancakes may be troublesome.

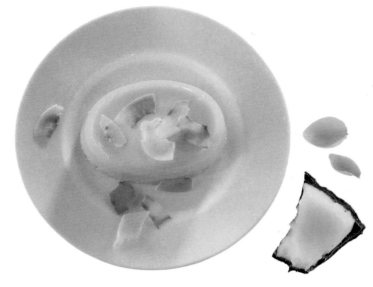

MANGO WITH STICKY RICE

COCONUT CUSTARD

225 g (8 oz/1¼ cups) sticky rice, soaked overnight in
    cold water
250 ml (8 fl oz/1 cup) coconut milk
pinch salt
2-4 tablespoons sugar, to taste
2 large ripe mangoes, peeled and halved
3 tablespoons coconut cream, see page 10
mint leaves to decorate

Drain and rinse rice thoroughly. Place in a
steaming basket lined with a double thickness
of muslin. Steam over simmering water for 30
minutes. Remove from heat.

3 eggs
2 egg yolks
500 ml (16 fl oz/2 cups) coconut milk
85 g (3 oz/⅓ cup) caster sugar
few drops rosewater or jasmine essence
toasted cocnut, to decorate

Preheat the oven to 180C (350F/Gas 4).
Place 4 individual heatproof dishes in a
baking tin.

In a bowl, stir together coconut milk, salt and
sugar to taste until sugar has dissolved. Stir in
warm rice. Set aside for 30 minutes.

In a bowl, stir together eggs, egg yolks,
coconut milk, sugar and rosewater or jasmine
essence until sugar dissolves. Pass through a
sieve into dishes. Pour boiling water into
baking tin to surround dishes.

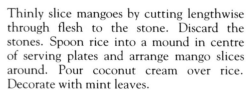

Thinly slice mangoes by cutting lengthwise
through flesh to the stone. Discard the
stones. Spoon rice into a mound in centre
of serving plates and arrange mango slices
around. Pour coconut cream over rice.
Decorate with mint leaves.

Serves 4.

Cook in oven for about 20 minutes until
custards are lightly set in centre. Remove
from baking tin and allow to cool slightly
before unmoulding. Serve warm or cold.
Decorate with coconut.

Serves 4.

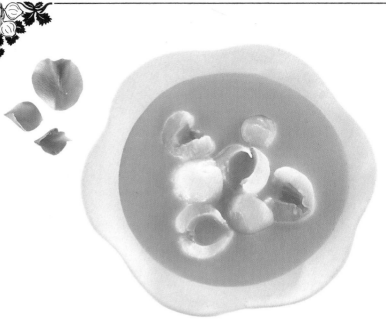

LYCHEES & COCONUT CUSTARD

GOLDEN THREADS

3 egg yolks
3-4 tablespoons caster sugar
200 ml (7 fl oz/scant 1 cup) coconut milk
85 ml (3 fl oz/⅓ cup) coconut cream, see page 10
about 1 tablespoon triple-distilled rose water
red food colouring
**about 16 fresh lychees, peeled, halved and stones
    removed**
rose petals, to decorate

In a bowl, whisk together egg yolks and sugar.

6 egg yolks
1 teaspoon egg white
450 g (1 lb/2 cups) sugar
few drops jasmine essence

Strain egg yolks through muslin into a small bowl. Beat lightly with egg white. In a saucepan, gently heat sugar, jasmine essence and 250 ml (8 fl oz/1 cup) water, stirring until sugar dissolves, then boil until thickened slightly. Adjust heat so syrup is hot but not moving.

In a medium, preferably non-stick, saucepan, heat coconut milk to just below boiling point, then slowly stir into bowl. Return to pan and cook very gently, stirring with a wooden spoon, until custard coats the back of the spoon.

Spoon a small amount of egg yolk into a piping bag fitted with a very fine nozzle or a cone of greaseproof paper with very small hole in pointed end. Using a circular movement, carefully dribble a trail into syrup, making swirls about 4-5 cm (1½-2 in) in diameter with a small hole in centre. Make a few at a time, cooking each briefly until set.

Remove from heat and stir in coconut cream, rose water to taste and sufficient red food colouring to colour pale pink. Leave until cold, stirring occasionally. Spoon a thin layer of rose-flavoured custard into 4 small serving bowls. Arrange lychees on custard. Decorate with rose petals. Serve remaining custard separately to pour over lychees.

Serves 4.

Using a skewer inserted in hole in centre of spiral, transfer each nest to a plate. Continue making similar nests with remaining egg yolks. When nests are cool, arrange on a serving plate.

Serves 4.

INDEX